WHAT THEY DIDN'T TEACH ME
IN SUNDAY SCHOOL

Also by Rob Parsons

Loving Against the Odds
The Sixty Minute Father
The Sixty Minute Marriage
The Sixty Second Father

What they didn't teach me in Sunday School

. . . Lessons I wish I'd learnt earlier

Rob Parsons

Hodder & Stoughton
LONDON   SYDNEY   AUCKLAND

Copyright © 1997 by Rob Parsons

First published in Great Britain in 1997

3 5 7 9 10 8 6 4 2

A CIP catalogue record for this title is available
from the British Library

ISBN 0 340 64276 9

Typeset by Palimpsest Book Production Limited,
Polmont, Stirlingshire
Printed and bound in Great Britain by
Clays Ltd, St Ives plc

Hodder and Stoughton Ltd
A division of Hodder Headline PLC
338 Euston Road
London NW1 3BH

To John Loosemore – who believed in me.

Contents

Before we start . . .

Just before I wrote my first book somebody warned me
that it was like giving birth – a strange mixture of pain
and joy. They said the problem with publishers is that
when you meet them, you want to know how your
last baby is doing, but they want to know if you're
pregnant! I have now given birth to five books, but,
unlike in my real family, I have a favourite. Some
of you may have read the 'Sixty Minute' books on
marriage and parenting. I loved writing those books
and they are special to me. People from all walks of
life, in multitudes of different situations, and with all
shades of belief and non-belief, have written to say those
books helped them; I am grateful for that. But it will not
take you long to realise that this book is different. Here
I share my deepest beliefs. Many of them have been
carved out of times of pain and disappointment but each
is precious to me.

I completely understand that your views may be
different to mine, or you may have no religious beliefs

at all, but here are the things that matter to me. I have told my two children that if in years to come, long after I am gone, they ever forget what mattered most to their father they can find it in this book. Here is my heart. This is my favourite child.

So many people have helped me give birth! First of all thank you to my Sunday School teachers; the older I get the more I appreciate what you gave me. Thanks also to Jonathan Booth, Lyndon Bowring, Charlie Colchester, Sheron Rice, Tom Beardshaw, Lisa Curtis, Kate Hancock, Dr R. T. Kendall, Louise Kendall, Elizabeth McCusker, Peter Mortimer and Steve Williams. Special thanks to Charles Nettleton, Judith Longman and the team at Hodder and Stoughton who always seem ready to go the extra mile.

As ever, special thanks and love to Dianne, Katie, Lloyd and Ron.

Introduction

I was four years old when Miss Williams called for me. My parents didn't go to church but had enlisted me in the Sunday School of the church on the corner of our street. During my time there many teachers would look after me, but Miss Williams, who supervised the infants' class, was the first.

Just recently that church celebrated its hundredth anniversary and the members invited me to say a few words at a Thanksgiving service. As I sat waiting to take part, my eyes gazed around the building. The old pews are long since gone and the large pulpit was taken down years ago, but so much was still the same. As I allowed my mind to wander back down the years, the walls whispered their memories to me. Let me mention just two.

Sometimes our teacher would invite the class to tea on a Sunday. My mother used to start preparing me for that occasion on the previous Monday. We didn't have a bathroom but the old tin bath would be dragged in from the garden, more times that week than in the previous month. As the moment drew closer she would try to put a small boy through the equivalent of a Swiss finishing school.

Finally the time would come – 3.45 on a Sunday afternoon. She would dampen my hair for the fifteenth time, thrust one of my father's handkerchiefs into my pocket and pass on a final word of exhortation. I can quite understand that at such a moment there are a million things a mother might want to say to her son; after all, he was leaving home for two hours to have tea with the Sunday School teacher. It often seemed that the responsibility of a last piece of advice would fluster her, and it would normally come down to, 'Remember, if there's just one sandwich left – leave it.'

Oh those teas! Marmite sandwiches, jelly, blanc-mange and cup cakes. A grace that seemed never to stop and a television, on that day at least, that never started. But I loved those times. My teacher was saying to me, 'You are special. I care enough about you to invite you into my home – away from the varnished pews and the canvas-backed hymn books – into my private world.'

And then there was the Sunday School Outing. I can remember praying so hard the night before, that it would be fine. My young mind didn't consider that ten thousand farmers may have been praying for rain. In any event what did the national wheat harvest matter when you put it up against the Sunday School Outing? It may be hard for a modern child to understand the wonder of that event. I confess that, as I look back, even I can't quite remember why the prospect of running around a muddy field and dining on a bun and a glass of milk held such excitement.

But as I sat in church on that anniversary day other memories came flooding back. These were not the memories of the child in Sunday School but of the man. In the middle of a slide presentation I suddenly saw myself aged seven at a Sunday School party. As I gazed at the child in the photograph I could not help but think, 'He had no idea what lay ahead; no notion of the pain and joys that were to come.' In truth, when I left Sunday School I had no idea that the learning process was only just beginning.

The lessons that lay ahead of me were not listed in any Sunday School curriculum, nor did they come packaged in a 'How to be a successful Christian' home study course. No, these lessons creep up on us. Sometimes they ambush us. Many of them are learnt through pain and some through apparent failure. With some of them I hardly realised I was back in school.

When the anniversary service was over I walked down the aisle to make my way out. As I did so a silver-haired lady made her way to me and asked,

'Do you remember me?'

'Yes – of course!' I said.

To my eye she seemed to have changed so little since she collected me on that Sunday afternoon all those years ago.

Miss Williams and those faithful people that came

3

after her taught me well, but these pages contain some of the lessons I could not learn in Sunday School. There are, of course, other lessons, not mentioned here, but each of those that follow has been significant for me, and not a few of them life-changing. Many of these lessons were learnt over many years and some of them the hard way. It is probably true that the lessons we learn hardest we learn best, yet it need not always be that way. I wish with all my heart I could have learnt some of them earlier and a little easier. And I don't presume that my lessons will be as important in your life as they have been in mine – but they just might be. And, if they are, this little book could save you years.

To live our lives looking over our shoulders asking, 'What do others think of me?' is a wearying way to exist. But this trauma does not only affect those who feel inadequate; many successful men and women live in the prison of other people's opinions of their lives. And it is a prison indeed, for it robs us of freedom in our social and family life, our careers and in our very spirits.

1

The greatest freedom is in having nothing to prove

It all began in the nursery. Claire was just six months old when the toothless face leant over the cot and said, 'Smile for grandad.' Claire did not feel like smiling; she'd had an awful night. Every time she whimpered her parents had leapt into her bedroom, yanked her out of the cot and started to bounce her up and down. And this morning had begun badly. The usual milk was apparently off the menu and instead they had served up something that, if she hadn't been sure her parents loved her, she could have sworn was stewed prunes. Claire was not happy.

Nevertheless the toothless old gentleman still called down to her, 'Smile for me!' She was just about to throw a heavy rattle at the old man when she felt the wind in her stomach and her face involuntarily broke into a huge grin. And it was then that something happened which was to affect the whole of Claire's life. Her grandfather yelled, 'She's done it! She smiled for me.' As a reward he passed down a cuddly toy to her and then rushed off to get other adults to witness the phenomenon. Soon there was only standing room around the cot as various members of the family stared down, hoping for a repeat of the wonder.

Claire gazed up, thought, 'Why not?' – and broke into a wide smile. The crowd went wild – they clapped, patted her on the head, and, most important of all, inundated the cot with goodies.

At the tender age of six months, eleven days, and fourteen hours, Claire Emma Taylor had learnt a lesson that was to mould her whole life: *You can make people like you by what you do; it really is possible to earn love.*

Most of us never manage to completely unlearn that lesson and when we are finally laid to rest it is at the end of a life that has been dominated by the desire, and even the need, to prove ourselves to somebody. By that time the sheer effort involved in that pursuit has left us physically and emotionally exhausted; before we slip away we have only strength for one last thought – 'I wonder how many people will come to my funeral?'

Some years ago two cardiologists, Friedman and Rosenman, set out to discover why some people were more prone to heart attack than others. That study led to their discovery of the now famous 'Type A' person. In some ways their research held few surprises; the Type A personality was often a 'make it happen' character that lived life at a furious pace, but there was at least one fascinating find. They discovered that the lifestyle adopted by these people was often heavily influenced by two personality characteristics.

The first was that such people have a keen sense of

the brevity of life – 'I'm forty-nine years old. In another fifty-one years I'll be a hundred. It's already April. It's ten to three! Where is life going?' Because of this, these people are consumed with the notion of making the best use of their time. Sadly this often doesn't mean using their time effectively; rather it involves jamming as many activities as possible into any given block of time. We find them on the phone to a friend at the same time as reading a bed-time story to their child; we catch them frantically trying to dial a number whilst doing ninety miles an hour on a motorway; we observe them listening to motivational tapes whilst lying on the beach on holiday.

Many of the people that Friedman and Rosenman examined were very successful men or women and I often wonder if they were surprised at the second characteristic which they found – *low self-esteem and the need to prove themselves*.

It was this characteristic that so often led to these people living *driven* lives. They worked long hours – irrespective of the need – were insanely competitive (they would find themselves desperately trying to win a game of Monopoly with a five-year-old), and were constantly asking themselves, 'What do other people think of me?' They hardly knew it but they had come to believe that the only way to be accepted – even loved – was to perform well. The strange thing was that success did not fulfil that need; rather, it fuelled it as they were driven to prove themselves in even greater tasks. Failure, or even a little criticism, could crush them utterly.

I have learnt that being a Christian does not necessarily exempt us from this kind of lifestyle. I have lived it for much of my life and even now, although its hold seems weaker, it is, for me, an ongoing battle. But battle it is, for this way of living can not only kill your body, but has the ability slowly to strangle your inner spiritual life. This is how one man put it:

Work had always been highly esteemed in our family, and hard work was seen as the primary tool for success. I figured if it was good to work ten hours, it would be even better to work fourteen . . .

I would come home feeling that I hadn't worked enough. So I tried to cram even more into my schedule . . . My life wasn't abundant, it was a frantic sprint from one hour to the next.

I can remember times when fatigue left me feeling isolated and alienated – feelings that previously had been foreigners to me . . . I became frustrated and laughter, which had always been my most treasured companion, had silently slipped away.

I was dominated by 'shoulds' and 'ought to's' and 'musts'. I would awaken unrefreshed in the morning, with a tired kind of resentment, and hurry through the day trying to uncover and meet the demands of others. Days were not lived but endured. I was exhausted trying to be a hope constantly rekindled for others, straining to live up to their images of me. I had worked hard to build up a reputation as one who was concerned, available, and involved – now I was being tyrannized by it. Often I was more at peace in the eyes of others than in my own.

Hurry needs answers; answers need categories; categories need labelling and dissecting. The pace I was trying to maintain had no time for rhythm and awe, for mystery and wonder . . . In order to keep up my incessant activity, God was simply reduced to fit into my schedule. I suffered because he didn't fit.[1]

Such a person is often popular and that very popularity can so often mask the great tragedy going on in the heart. We have managed to build a reputation as a man or woman who gets things done. We are in demand to sit on committees, to organise functions, to teach Sunday School, to do anything and everything. We have long since given up going to church to worship. No, we go now to push agendas forward; there are people to see, things to organise. As the preacher speaks we are jotting down the names of the people we need to see when the service is over but we need not have worried, for even as we open our eyes after the final prayer, there is a long line of people wanting a minute of our time. We are needed. The word that is always on our lips is, 'Yes'.

'Yes, of course I can sit on that committee.'

'Yes, I'd be pleased to help in any way I can.'

'You only have to ask – you know I'd love to help.'

In truth we are back in the nursery yelling to anyone who will listen, 'I'm smiling – come and see me smile. I am trying hard to make you love me.'

The great tragedy of this situation is that so often whilst we are saying 'Yes' to the whole world, we are saying 'No' to those who need us most. I have made so many mistakes in this area. I remember being so busy when the children were small that I just didn't have time for my own family. Was I popular? You'd better believe it! At times I could almost hear people saying, 'Oh, he's such a gifted speaker. He's so willing to help. He's always there when we need him.' And that might have been fine had the great speaker spent a little more time communicating with his own family. It might have been acceptable if the one who was so willing to help others had heard his own wife's cries for help a little earlier, and if the man who was 'always there when we need him' had been more available to those for whom he had primary responsibility.

Some years ago I received an anonymous letter from a church leader's wife. It contained a poem. She has never known how often I have read it and cried in my heart for her. It moves me because I have no doubt this woman loves her husband but he has no idea what his busy life is doing to their relationship. She is reaching out from her very soul:

I want my husband to smile again.
I want to be able to talk to him after dinner.
I want for our family to go out on Saturdays for a
    walk or a shopping trip.
I want to be me – not 'the minister's wife'.

I want to sit in church, listen to the notices, and
    decide what *I would like to go to.*
I want my husband to come home at night and
    relax instead of just recharging the batteries
    and disappearing out again.
I want to celebrate birthdays and anniversaries
    always, not just when there are no church
    meetings.
I want to be able to tell the self-centred and
    self-righteous folk that they are.
I want him to come in at night and talk to us
    instead of slumping silently reliving the awkward
    visit or difficult meeting he's been at.
I want people to stop telling me how wonderful
    it must be to be the minister's wife and then
    complain they've not had a visit for months.
I want people who regularly miss meetings
    because they've 'had a busy day' to let us miss
    occasional meetings because we've 'had a
    busy day'.
I want him to come with me sometimes to see our
    child swim or play football.
I want him to be my husband instead of their
    minister.
And I want not to be guilty about these things.[2]

At the bottom of the poem is a PS, 'Tonight is one of
those nights when it is all too much for me. I hope that
you will read this and maybe pray for us even though you
don't know us.'

13

Who is this woman who has written to a stranger with such a cry from the heart? Where does she live, and is life better for her and their child now? Is her husband still so busy, and is this busyness producing fruit or barrenness?

A lifestyle of busyness and over-commitment has one particular characteristic: whatever we do, it will never be enough. I once received a letter from a woman who described what she called 'the agony' of trying to be the 'perfect mother' in the eyes of her in-laws. One would have thought that those of us who live this way would be thrilled when we achieve a goal. And we are – for a very *little* while. Somebody compliments us on a job we have done and we feel a fleeting glow of pleasure, but almost immediately an inner voice whispers, 'Will I do the next job as well?' We may be a church leader and smile as the member of the congregation says, 'I enjoyed your sermon today; God spoke to me.' But as she moves away and we extend our hand to greet the next person, an inner voice asks, 'Will I be as compelling next week?' In truth, whether we are church leaders, students, sales executives or homemakers we are constantly asking ourselves, 'Can I go on pleasing you – will you approve of me tomorrow?'

The constant need to prove ourselves, to earn acceptance and even love is utterly draining. Those of us caught on its treadmill have no resting place for we must always be on to the next thing. We know little satisfaction at what we have achieved. We have no inner peace. We even feel guilty when we try to relax. Holidays are often not an oasis but something to be endured until we can get back to the security of activity. I remember one church leader confiding to me that he worried if he went to the park with his wife and children in an afternoon in case a member of his congregation saw him and thought he was shirking. The fact that he works evenings and all day Sunday and rarely takes holidays didn't figure in his thinking. He is in the prison of 'What they will think?' and, although it is sad, I understand it completely – I've spent a sentence or two there myself.

The symptoms of the driven life – distorted sense of worth, restlessness of spirit, inability to enjoy success or even to relax – are miserable enough. But there is a greater, more terrifying, factor in the driven life; such a person has the ability to run on empty for years. Long after the reality of faith has died in the heart and years after any real sense of communion with God has gone, the driven life prays, sings, organises, preaches, gives financially – in fact does anything that involves 'doing' rather than 'being'. The great tragedy is that whilst others are fooled he or she is usually not so deluded. They know what has happened; they have died inside.

Their first day in heaven

The three of them were at the gates,
all togged up in their new wings.
'I wonder if we'll sing?' said Herbert.
Mrs Gee and Herbert looked at their heavenly

mate and Herbert said in his Sunday
voice,
'My name is Herbert Hodgkinson – deacon at the
    South Sea Mission,
Chairman of the Billy Graham inter-college
    Christian Union,
Sunday School inspector for the whole of
    Yorkshire East,
Co-ordinator of the Federation of British Whitsun
    Treats,
Teacher, preacher, evangelizer, prophet, priest
    and . . .'

'My name's Bartholomew. On earth I knew . . .'
'Pleased to meet you!' came the rushing wind of
    Mrs Gee,
organiser of the local 'Save the Natives tea',
Women's Guild and sewing class,
Christian croquet on the grass.
Healthy, red and rosy, she.

'My name's Bartholomew,' said he,
'On earth I knew . . .'

'You ever preached at Bognor Hall?'

'I never preached nowhere at all.'

'Does your wife arrange flowers for the local
    church?'

'No . . . left me and three kids years ago – left us
    in the lurch.'

And Mrs Gee turned to dear Herb and said,
'Why this is strange and so absurd.
This little man with scars, and wounds and
  dirty face.
I must say, Herb, he's out of place.
And blood all over his new wings.
It shows a life of awful sins . . .'

But then *He* came.
A light so bright that all three cringed before the
  King of Heaven.

It was Herbert who recovered first and soon
  began his usual burst:
'I'm Herbert Hodgkinson, chairman . . .'
'And I'm Mrs Gee, *surely* you remember me.'

But then He spoke, 'Bartholomew, it's good to see
  you. Come with me.'

And Mrs Gee quite red with rage turned on St
  Peter to complain,
'Why him? Why him? It's so absurd?'

'Shhh . . . they knew each other . . . back
  on earth.'

Can we change? Yes, but it is not an easy road. We do
not easily give up the security of the life that earns its
approval, and even its love, by doing. Sometimes what
causes us to change is the welfare of those around us. It
may be that a close family member, perhaps our husband

or wife, begins to crack under the strain. The strange thing is that those of us living a frantic lifestyle often cope reasonably well for a while; it is those around us who pick up the real cost. I have seen many people begin the search for a different way to live when they have seen what the present style is doing to those they love.

And some change because of illness. The headaches, the stomach pain, the irritability and the hostility that so often accompanies this way of life, gradually increase, and finally our body says 'enough'. And now we have to be quiet, perhaps even confined to bed, and this gives us time to do the one thing that most of us manage to avoid for a lifetime – we begin to think.

Some time ago, at a seminar I was running, I met a lawyer. He told me that a car crash in which he had almost lost his life and which left him hospitalised for six months, changed him completely. He said, 'I used to carry photographs of my children around to remind myself what they looked like. But the office survived without me, and I began to see the things that really mattered to me.' This is how one church leader described such an experience:

On Tuesday I picked up my diary to review the week's schedule: four seriously ill people to call on, my own doctor's appointment, several requests for counselling, a sermon outline for the church bulletin to be completed by tomorrow morning, a fund-raising letter to be written to the congregation by Thursday, five meetings scheduled between

Tuesday evening and Friday noon. On Friday night and Saturday I was speaking three times to our leadership training class, on Sunday preaching twice. My Sunday sermon was, 'Doing what you can', but I knew I was way beyond that. I survived the week by postponing some visiting, giving up my day off and cancelling two meetings. My wife said, 'You have made this church your mistress.' But what could I give up? How could I change?

He then became seriously ill and thought that he might lose his life. He spoke of that experience:

I have never had so much time to think, and the words that came repeatedly to my mind were limits and finitude. The conflict between my racing mind and wild emotions and helpless body forced me to realise that if I were going to live and recover my ministry my priorities required a major overhaul. What did God want to teach me about a different style of life and ministry?[3]

Some years ago I was battling over these same issues: I wanted peace yet desperately needed the affirmation I thought I'd find through sheer activity. Then a friend showed me something he had just read. I didn't know the author but he had written about me:

When I took a closer look at this I realised that I was caught in a strange web of paradoxes.

Whilst complaining about too many demands, I felt
  uneasy when none were made.
Whilst speaking about the burden of letter writing,
  an empty mailbox made me sad.
Whilst fretting about giving lecture tours, I felt
  disappointed when there were no invitations.
Whilst speaking nostalgically about an empty
  desk, I feared the day when that would
  come true.
In short, whilst desiring to be alone, I was
  frightened of being left alone.
The more I became aware of these paradoxes, the
  more I started to see how much I had indeed
  fallen in love with my own compulsions and
  illusions, and how much I needed to step back
  and wonder, 'Is there a quiet stream underneath
  the fluctuating affirmations and rejections of my
  little world? Is there a still point where my life is
  anchored and from which I can reach out with
  hope and courage and confidence?'[4]

For some of us the journey towards finding that 'quiet
stream' begins in tears but also with a burning passion to
find a better way to live. It has been said that the greatest
freedom is in having nothing to prove, but so often this
involves a lesson even harder to learn than being free of
proving ourselves to each other. We need to be free of
proving ourselves to God. It's the next lesson.

I heard of a man who as a boy never felt affirmed by his father. As the boy became a man he realised that his father's critical spirit made him wonder if he had ever been accepted as a son.

He was in his mid-forties and married with children of his own, when one day his father, whom he had not seen for five years, telephoned to say he was about to visit. He panicked; he now had a beard and he knew his father would not approve. The old man was due to arrive in five days' time and on each of those days the son argued with himself over whether or not he should shave off his beard. He found himself talking to himself – 'You're a father yourself now. You must make your own decisions.' But at ten o'clock in the morning on the day his father was due to arrive, he shaved off his beard.

He waited on a crowded platform and suddenly saw his father walking towards him. He smiled and went to shake his father's hand but hesitated as he saw the old man's brow furrow. His father said, 'Nice to see you son. But aren't those sideburns a little long?'

At that very moment he knew that nothing had changed. This was still the man he could not please. Many of us have lived our Christian lives as though God is a father like that. The day we discover differently is the day we begin to live.

This could be your day.

2

I am known completely and loved unconditionally

I have spoken to thousands of people during the coffee breaks in our seminars but for some reason my conversation with one man remains as clear as if it were yesterday. He was about forty years old. He said, 'I'm a director of a company, I have two hundred people working for me, I have three children of my own. By most standards people look at me and say that I'm successful.' And then he dropped his voice and whispered, 'Tell me why I am still trying to prove myself to my father.' He told me that when he was a teenager he had come running in from school anxious to tell his father that he had come second in a music examination that included candidates from the whole of his county. His father had listened to his son's enthusiasm and then asked, 'Won't you ever come first?'

Many Christians live like that man. They believe that God is their father, they believe they came into that relationship because of faith. If you asked them whether it is possible to earn God's love they would tell you they are trusting in the grace of God. But in reality they spend their lives trying to earn that love. God becomes for them the father they can never please, the one who always has another demand up his sleeve, the one they are forever disappointing.

These people have forgotten the number of times they have rededicated their lives to God, and their bookshelves bear evidence to the efforts of the years to find the magic formula which will turn them into the kind of Christian that God will be proud of. There have been times when they have risen from bed before it was light and prayed until their knees hurt, and moments when they have almost read the Bible in a year, but even then he seemed to want more.

One man wrote to me and put it like this:

I attend church as well as another class every Sunday. I read the Bible and pray wherever I am, I go to prayer and praise at our minister's house every Wednesday and to another meeting on a Monday evening. Do I sound like a good Christian? This question has really puzzled me so I hope you will be able to help me. I am trying hard to be a good Christian and I'm more than ever involved in the church. Do you think I am doing enough? Thank you for taking the time to listen to me.[5]

I have tried to imagine this man striving hard to please God but all the time there is the nagging doubt that he will never be good enough. I have no doubt he listens to good preachers, reads helpful books and determines to progress in his faith, but there is rarely a sense of God's approval. If nobody helps him he will die wondering if he ever really made it.

I once saw a school photograph that saddened me deeply. It was of a large group of children at the beginning of their teen years. The girls were already looking like women in the making, the boys like . . . large boys. But one girl caught my attention. She was very overweight and sat with her hands on her knees. She did not have a pretty face, but she smiled out from behind thick spectacles. I asked my friend's child to tell me about her.

Apparently, she had few friends because, amongst other things, she smelt a little and some of the children would not sit by her. She was not good at sport and regularly came somewhere near the bottom of the class in terms of academic achievement. Whenever the teacher asked two leaders to pick teams, she was always the last one chosen and invariably one captain would say, 'You can have her.'

And as I looked at her, I felt a great emotion well up in me. I wanted to hold her, to tell her that she was *somebody*. I wanted to find something in that child's life that she could do moderately well and praise her for it. I wanted to tell her I would always be her friend, and I would love to sit next to her.

Not long ago I received a poem. It is called 'Picking Teams'.

When we pick teams in the playground
Whatever the game might be
There's always somebody left till last
And usually it's me.

I stand there looking hopeful
And tapping myself on the chest
But the captains pick the others first
Starting of course with the best.

Maybe if teams were sometimes picked
Starting with the worst
Once in his life a boy like me
Could end up being first.[6]

One child put it like this: 'Heaven is a place where there are no teams and nobody ever gets picked last.'

But many of us have never left the playground; we still secretly believe that God will only love us when we do well. The mind-blowing concept of grace – God's unmerited favour towards us – is hard for us to grasp in a society used to earning love. The truth is that the message of the gospel is a surprise; it runs counter to much we have been taught and almost all that we have experienced in other relationships. *God knows you and God loves you. He loved you when you were his enemy and he loves you now you are his child.*

Many of us find it hard to live in the good of this and so struggle all our lives trying to earn the very love of God. But when we live that way we are destined to live a weary Christian life, for proving yourself to God is the most draining lifestyle of all. When we reach extremes of this position it is hard even to believe that God is on our side. Only those who have woken each day with the daunting prospect of earning God's love have known the trauma of trying to achieve it.

I was a Christian for many years before I realised this. I used to live my Christian life as though God was constantly looking over the balcony of heaven just waiting for me to prove myself to him.

Some days I would feel as though I had done pretty well. I'd prayed, been gracious to the miserable man in the office next to me, and made the evening meeting at church. But as I fell into bed at the end of such a day did I feel liberated? No, it had been a long hard slog and I knew in my heart that I probably wouldn't be as 'spiritual' the next day.

And then one day somebody gave me some news that changed my life. He said the simple words, 'God is *for* you! He's for you when you succeed and when you fail. He's for you when your heart is filled with certainty and your head is filled with doubt. He's for you when you share the faith with thousands and when you deny him. God is for you – *He is on your side!*'

Now there's a revolutionary thought – *God is on our side.* The Bible tells us that nothing will ever separate us from the love of God – demons can't and angels won't.[7] Does he want us to spend time in prayer, to get to church meetings and to share our faith with others? Yes, but if we do them all he could not love us more, and if we miss them all he will not love us less.

This concept is so alien to our culture it is almost a daily battle to keep hold of it. But once we grasp it we find weights we have carried for many years begin to fall away. Somebody described it like this, 'Suddenly I felt an incredible freedom. It had dawned on me I did not have to prove myself to God. I not only felt loved, but a fresh love for him rising in me. How could I not love someone who had loved me unconditionally?'

I was at the door of the auditorium, shaking hands with people as they left, when she came up to me. I had been talking about the power of unconditional love and it was obvious that something I had said had touched this woman's heart but I am in her debt, for the story she told me that day has never left me.

She was a single parent and her son was twenty-three years old. She had tried hard to encourage him in the Christian faith and he used to go to church but somebody had offended him and he had stopped attending. She told me her son was a punk rocker. In fact he was the most outrageous punk rocker in the whole of her city. His head was shaved apart from a piece in the centre which stood up like the tail of a cockatoo and was bright orange. He wore a ring through his nose and cheek. He dressed in leather and wore a little mascara.

The previous week he had been helping her shop in a local supermarket and they were at the check-out when he said, 'I'm going to get some cigarettes then I'll come back and help you pack.' The moment he had left, the woman at the check-out said, 'How can you bear to be seen out with him when he looks like that?' The single-parent mum said to me, 'I smiled at her and said, "Oh, my dear, it's very easy. You see, I have brought him up through all these years. I love him. *He's my son.*"'

We can be moved by a story like this but it is still hard to believe that the God who knows us intimately – better than we know ourselves – should love us in such a way.

Some years ago a friend called at my home; he knew that I was going through a very difficult time. It was a Sunday morning and he asked if I minded missing church. I said, 'Not at all.' We talked together about handling criticism and how it was possible to feel of no value. And it was then that he said something that has remained with me until today. He told me there were lots of rumours spreading across the country about him. They were untrue, tiresome and hurtful. One night he had cried out to God, 'Lord, these rumours are hurtful!' And it was then he felt God say to him: 'They're not as bad as the truth; *and I know the truth and I still love you.*'

One night I gave a closing address at a Christian conference. I had preached on the fact that God knows the worst about us and yet loves us unconditionally – that he is our father. When I had finished I took my seat alongside the two men who were chairing the event. And then one of them made his way towards the microphone and told a most powerful story. Here is the event Jeff Lucas spoke of that night, as told in his book *Walking Backwards*:

I picked up the phone and my fears were confirmed:

Dad was dying. I was to cancel everything and rush home immediately on the next plane . . . Two hours later, I rushed into Dad's hospital room. He was conscious and, as I took his hand and smoothed his hair, he smiled but said nothing. My dad had been unable to speak for some four years. He loved to talk but that gift had been taken from him by a stroke which reduced his speech to meaningless drivel.

Now, as I sat at his bedside, I knew that time was short. 'Dad, I love you so very much. You know that don't you?' He smiled, but then his eyes clouded over. I could see he was struggling to say something important but the words wouldn't come out. However, he had overcome this handicap before. My dad knew how to communicate without words.

Some months earlier I'd been staying overnight at my parents' home. It was the end of the day and I had already retired to my room. There was a knock on the door. Dad came in and knelt down silently by the bed. He took the blankets and the sheets and tucked me in, just like he'd done thirty-five years earlier when I was his five-year-old. With a kiss on my cheek, brushing away a stray hair on my face, he was gone. I lay there in the dark, aware that here was I, a forty-year-old adult, so used to making decisions and fending for myself and my family, and I had just been tucked in and made warm and secure by my frail father. It felt good.[8]

Jeff then looked out at four thousand people and said, 'God wants to tuck some of you in tonight – to let you know again that you are loved.' As he spoke I watched the audience. I could both see and feel emotion bursting out all over the arena. Grown men and women were realising, some for the first time in their lives, that God loves them.

I have many close friends, some of whom I believe may even die for me. But they do not know me. They know parts of me and some of them may know me better than I know myself. But there is one who both knows me completely and yet loves me utterly. I am sometimes a disappointment to him, but never a surprise.

God is *for* you.

'Nothing succeeds like success.' We live in a society that loves winners. Almost every day we receive junk mail that promises to make us successful; there are seminars, books and videos that promise to help us reach that goal. The media worships at the altars of those who have made it and we drool at their lifestyles.

Nobody is ever going to write a best-seller called 'How to Fail – Ten steps to ensure you don't make it' and yet there is often a strange power at the heart of failure which can hold the key to greater success than we have ever dreamt of . . .

3

Tomorrow belongs to the failures

I will never forget the day it happened. My wife, Dianne, describes it like this:

> It was in so many ways a perfect morning. I had just woken and the sun was streaming into the room. I had a lovely home, a good marriage, and two beautiful children. The only problem was I had just turned to my husband and whispered, 'I don't think I can cope any more.' But things like this didn't happen to people like me; and in any event I couldn't let them happen. I had a little girl who needed me and a brand new baby, and I had a real faith in God. People like me didn't crack up – did they?

I remember Dianne saying, 'I can't take Katie to school today,' as though it were yesterday. I got up from bed and prepared Katie's breakfast before dropping her off at nursery school. I can't remember whether or not I thought this was going to be just a bad day, but, if I did, I was wrong. Something had affected Dianne's immune system causing her to sink into depression; whatever was going on in her life was not going to be solved overnight.

As the weeks turned into months I became more and more frustrated. I was, by now, a senior partner in a growing law practice, in demand as a speaker and up to my eyes in church leadership responsibilities. But the hardest thing of all was that I had no control over these circumstances that had suddenly hit our lives. In almost every other area of my life people came to me for help; I was the man who could make it happen, the person who could usually get the job done, the one you could rely on. But at home I was helpless. Worse still, the emotional aspect of what was happening to Dianne made it harder for some to sympathise. I got advice on how to be harder/softer/loving/tough. But nothing I did or didn't do made any difference. Dianne was ill.

I remember one night a leader from our church came to see me; he is a man with a big heart. I had just put the children to bed; Dianne was asleep upstairs. We talked for hours and then knelt in the darkness and prayed together. Suddenly I felt my shoulders begin to shake and I sobbed uncontrollably; none of the old resources worked in this situation. If I was wealthy I wasn't wealthy enough, if it was power I didn't have enough of it. I could only look up and ask God in his mercy to help us.

There is an old hymn which has these lines in it:

When we reach the end of our hoarded resources
Our Father's full giving has only begun.[9]

I have learnt that it is necessary in the life of the Kingdom to get to the end of those hoarded resources. These are the store of things on which we base our security. It could be our money, our talent, our position, our reputation. So long as we are relying on them we can achieve very little of lasting value. But there comes a time when we feel utter weakness, even failure, and at that moment we unleash a power so great it can overwhelm us. Jesus put it like this: 'Without me you can do nothing.'[10]

Those words do not mean that nothing is achieved. It is, unfortunately, possible to get a lot done without the presence or power of Jesus. We can organise meetings, build sanctuaries and write books without him. It means nothing of value – nothing that lasts for ever – gets done. But it is not the way of the Kingdom. And it is for this reason that time and time again the Bible shows us the power not of success . . . but of failure.

Let's take a vote. We have a hundred people in a room. Who is your favourite disciple? John gets fifteen because Jesus loved him especially; Andrew gets four because, although often in the background, he was always bringing people to Jesus; Thaddeus gets one because there is always somebody just dying to show you how clever they are; but Peter gets eighty. Why? . . . Because he failed. We love Peter because he reminds us of ourselves.

One of the most significant events in the life of Peter

37

occurred one night in the darkness on Lake Galilee.[11] The other disciples are in the boat but Jesus is not with them. Suddenly a storm rises up and then, through the storm, they see Jesus walking on the water. Peter calls out, 'Lord, I want to walk on the water with you!' The word that came back to him through the storm that night chilled him to the heart. Jesus said, 'Come!' and Peter climbed over the gunwale of the little boat and into the darkness.

I once saw a painting that depicted the event. It had captured the fact that Peter had lost his courage and begun to sink; it showed him up to his neck in water and about to drown. But that canvas is only half the story. *The other half is that Peter walked on the water.*

The critics will always be there. They will be sitting in the boat, perfectly dry and full of good advice as to how you got it wrong. But tomorrow belongs to those who are prepared to fail.

It was not long after the incident on Lake Galilee that Peter found himself in the big city – Jerusalem itself. It was just before dawn when it happened and the memory of two events never left him. The first was the sound of the cock crowing and the second was the look in the eyes of Jesus as he turned to him.[12] This was the very lowest point in his life. Days before, he had vowed to die with him; now, before sun-up, he was already on his third denial. Another of the disciples was to die that morning by his own hand – I wonder what kept Peter from doing the same? It may have been the conversation he had with the carpenter the night before. Jesus said, 'Simon,

Simon (Peter's old name), Satan has asked to sift you as wheat. But I have prayed for you, Simon, that your faith may not fail.'[13]

As Peter thought about that it must have struck him that there is hope beyond failure – the hope of strength beyond weakness. He didn't have to wait too long to discover the truth of this. The Sanhedrin was the most powerful court in the whole of Israel and when the young fisherman stood to address it and make his defence you would have found it hard to recognise the man who had denied the faith to a servant girl. He did not seem like Peter the denier when, refusing to stay quiet about the message of the risen Christ, he said, 'We cannot help speaking about what we have seen and heard.'[14]

And I have no doubt that Peter would occasionally come across a man or woman who would whisper to him in the market place, 'Yesterday I denied the Master.' And then they would hear some of the sweetest words we can ever hear from another human being: 'Me too.' 'You?' they would stutter, 'You denied him also?' And Peter would again relate how God uses not the successful but the weak; he has plans for the failures.

Shortly after Dianne became ill she said to me that because she wasn't well enough to go to church, she would like to start a small Bible study in our home. We called it 'The strugglers group.' It was for those who were spiritual waifs and strays, those on the edge. Some had no faith, others had lost the faith they once held dear. We seemed a strange duo to meet the needs of such people. All we had to offer was our weakness. I remember saying to one particularly bright social worker who was not a Christian, 'I'm sorry you haven't got a better example of Christianity to look at – we're going through a tough time at the moment.'

One night some months later this person left our home in a particularly difficult mood. The evening had not gone well; we had tried to share our faith as well as we could but she, in particular, was very negative. I said to Dianne, 'I doubt if Gill will ever find faith in Christ.' At one o'clock in the morning my telephone rang. It was she.

'He has met me,' she said.

'What happened?' I asked.

'After I left,' she replied, 'I drove home across the mountains and suddenly I felt tremendous love and forgiveness to some people who had hurt me badly. He met me! My heart is physically hurting. Will it be like this tomorrow?'

I remember saying, 'I don't know. It's never happened to me like that, but you are very fortunate. He has met you in a special way.'

It was just the firstfruits of a great harvest from that group. We saw people find faith for the first time, others rediscover a relationship with God they thought had gone for ever. Many of those who came are now in leadership roles themselves. What had been born in weakness was operating in a power I had never seen before.

You may be a great preacher, but be careful your gift does not get in the way of God moving in power. It would be better for you to stutter words that he wanted you to say than to preach your best sermon in your own strength. You may be wealthy; it is a great responsibility. You must come to the point where you realise that God does not need your money. He says, '. . . for every animal of the forest is mine, and the cattle on a thousand hills . . . If I were hungry I would not tell you.'[15] It is your privilege to use what you have in his Kingdom. And you must lay down the sense of control that wealth brings, for it will ruin you. You may be a great organiser – but spend time listening, as well as doing. Have God bring you to the place where you would rather organise a tea-party that he wants than arrange an international convention that a committee has dreamt up.

There is a very moving account at the beginning of Luke's Gospel.[16] Joseph and Mary had taken the boy Jesus, aged twelve, from the north down to Jerusalem to celebrate Passover. On the way back they suddenly realise that he is not with them and they begin to retrace their steps to find him. The Authorised Version of the Bible puts it very powerfully; 'But they, supposing him to have been in the company, went a day's journey . . . And when they found him not, they turned back again to Jerusalem, seeking him.'[17]

It can happen to us so easily in our careers, our ambitions, and our church activities. We blast ahead, relying on our gifts, our resources, and all seems to be well. But we have gone on wrongly assuming that Jesus was with us. It is truly frightening to consider what can be achieved without God being with us and too scary for words to think about what it all adds up to: *nothing*.

If we go on but don't realise that Jesus is not with us, one of two things normally happens. Sometimes God causes us to go through an experience that makes us feel again our need of him. I am sure that I would not be writing this book now if it were not for the fact of Dianne's illness all those years ago. The other possibility is we never know – we are too concerned with ourselves, with our success, with the next project, with all we must achieve, to realise that actually *we are on our own*.

Over the years people have often said to me, 'But isn't your faith in God a crutch?' I always answer in the same way, 'Yes. I think it is. But I was never meant to make it on my own. I was meant to lean on him.'

The world may admire success – and I can understand that – but its aim is too low.

Tomorrow belongs to the failures.

I've seen Tiger Woods hit a golf ball three hundred and fifty yards. I've watched McEnroe serve so that the opponent didn't see it, let alone return it. I've sat enthralled as Billy Graham has said, 'I want you to leave your seats,' and thousands have walked forward. And when one of my old Sunday School teachers told me the story of the flood I sometimes imagined that my feet were wet.

These people did not acquire these gifts overnight, and they were not developed without effort; but each of them had discovered the effectiveness, the liberation and the sheer power that occurs when you find the one thing at which you are gifted and do it with all your heart.

4

When you play to your strengths the giants fall faster

The belief that he could do it had risen slowly in his heart.[18] True, it was a greater feat than he had ever accomplished, and the possibility of becoming a laughing stock and losing his life in the process was very real. And yet he still believed.

It was that belief that caused him to push his way through the soldiers to the tent that stood in the middle of the encampment, and gave him the courage to actually speak the words, 'I want to see the king.'

The sergeant looked at him, smiled and said, 'Do you, lad? Now who shall I say it is that wants an audience?'

David saw the smile leave the soldier's face, and he could hardly believe that he had said it, but, yes, the words had come out of his mouth: 'Tell him it's the giant killer.'

And suddenly he, the shepherd boy, was face to face with the most powerful man in the whole of Israel. The prepared speech stuck in his throat, and all he could remember later was mumbling about killing a lion that had threatened his sheep. He waited: the King smiled. It was hard to discern if he was impressed or just desperate, but the King agreed – the boy could fight Goliath.

And then it happened – an event so innocuous, so lacking in maliciousness that David did not at first realise the danger that almost cost him his life. King Saul said, 'You can do it, but I want you to wear this.' The King nodded to a slave nearby and it was carried in. It was unmistakable – David had seen it from a distance, he knew people that had almost died in the crush to touch it. It looked impregnable, as if any man who wore it would become immortal. As the slave held it high, the sun shining through the tent flap caught it and momentarily blinded David. He, the least of all his brothers, was to wear Saul's armour.

Of course, David said, 'Yes.' He climbed into the huge metal gaiters, and waited patiently as the great iron breastplate was chained around his body. The helmet slid over his eyes and he had to hold it up to stop himself looking ridiculous. Two men lifted the sword and pressed it into his hands and it was all he could do to stop himself crying out at the pain of the weight that jarred his forearm. But finally it was done and he longed to be gone and get on with it. And he would have been gone, but he realised that he simply couldn't move.

Every face was on him, and he lowered his head in embarrassment. They knew. And then he saw it. One of the soldiers had ripped it from his belt as they had dressed him in the iron and it lay on the floor near the door of the tent. The leather that he had so painstakingly fashioned seemed old and listless compared to the gleam of the armour. And yet in a moment he knew what he must do. Later, as he remembered what he said to the King that day, he realised that it took at least as much courage to say it as to fight the giant, but it saved his life and, more importantly, allowed God to work.

'O King, there is no man in all of Israel I want to please more than you and no deed that means more to me than to kill the one who is pouring scorn on the God we serve, but I cannot wear your armour because I am not you. It may be hard for you to understand, but my real gift is in my sling. If you will just let me be me, I believe that God can do something that will amaze both of us.'

The King watched as the stone left the leather, and he hardly needed to follow its flight because it was all in the face of the boy – the faith, the gift . . . the freedom.

I was brought up on the story of Goliath, but I wish I'd understood the concept of 'Saul's armour' earlier. The principle is a very simple one but when we grasp it we find it to be life-changing. It is based on the fact that each of us has special gifts; these can be natural, like being good with numbers or sport, or spiritual, like preaching. The whole world may want to make us just like them, but when we operate within our own gifting, we not only see better results but, like David, improve our chances of achieving them without killing ourselves.

Let's say you have a gift of organising events. A large conference is coming up and somebody asks you to help. You have to raise some finance, plan the marketing and invite the speakers. You do it well. It's true it has taken the best part of six months and there have been hassles galore, but it's the day before the opening and it's ready to go.

And then somebody on the committee asks if you would mind saying a few words on the opening night. As they speak you can feel your heart-rate increase and you begin to sweat. You hate public speaking, and know that if you grant the request you will spend the next twenty-four hours worrying and practising and probably make a mess of it anyway. You know for sure that this is not a task you should undertake and so you say – *'Yes, of course I'd love to help'*!

It's important to realise what went on in that situation. At the very moment you said 'Yes' you laid down your real gift. Like David's sling, it fell to the floor. That would have been bad enough, but you also climbed right into Saul's armour. You're no public speaker – and you know it – but you wanted to please somebody, you wanted to do your bit and perhaps there was even a little conceit at being asked. But beware, you are soon to be on top of a hill with a giant to kill and totally immobile!

Gift is a strange thing. It's very important that at some stages of our lives, and in order to discover our real gifts, we try things that we are pretty sure aren't our talents. There is many a man or woman whose primary gift is something they were once terrified of doing. That is not the same as spending *a lifetime* trying to do things that, for us, are 'Saul's armour'. And having discovered our gifts it's vital that so far as is possible *we play to our strengths*. The problem is that life is full of people who either want you to be just like them or seem determined to turn you into *their* idea of perfection. If you and I listen to them at least three things will happen: first, we'll become just like them – tearing around saying 'yes' to the whole world and losing our sanity in the bargain; next, we'll be so busy fulfilling other people's expectations of our life that we'll never get round to finding out what God may have had planned for us; and lastly, not only will we never develop our God-given gifts, but we'll get in the way of others developing theirs.

But you could well say, 'You should come to my church. It's not exactly that we've got people rushing round grabbing other people's opportunities – we can't get anybody to do anything.' That may be true, but it's still no reason for you to do *everything*.

I wonder why we find it so difficult to say 'No' to those who ask us to help, even if this leads us into a life of crushing busyness in which we become totally ineffective. I can't help but believe part of the answer lies in a phrase that we don't hear much of today – 'the call of God' on our lives. When we have no real sense of that call, no certainty of what we are meant to be saying 'Yes' to, it makes it hard to say 'No' to anything.

Somebody said to me years ago that Jesus achieved all he did in three short years because he did what his father told him to do. He had a clear understanding of what he was meant to be saying 'Yes' to. The practical results in his life were that at times he knew it was right to say 'No'.

'Will you be our king?' – 'No.'[19]

'Will you settle this dispute between my brother and Me?' – 'No.'[20]

'Will you come back to Capernaum?' – 'No. Let us go somewhere else . . . so I can preach there also.'[21]

Most of us are 'Yes' people. We long to be needed and we crave to be liked, but we pay the price of never knowing the achievements and peace of those who have the security to play to their strengths – to listen to the call. Euripides put it like this: 'The same man cannot well be skilled in everything – each has his own special excellences.' Those 'special excellences' are vital. Paul gets to the heart of the issue when he says, 'If the whole body were an eye, where would the sense of hearing be?'[22]

It's never too late to change – but hurry! Quentin Crisp was right: 'It's no good running a pig farm badly for thirty years while saying, "Really I was meant to be a ballet dancer." By that time pigs will be your style.'

Let the rabbits run

Imagine there is a meadow. In that meadow there is a duck, a fish, an eagle, a squirrel and a rabbit.

They decide they want to have a school so they can be clever just like people.

With the help of some grown-up animals, they come up with a curriculum they believe will make a well-rounded animal:

Running

Swimming

Tree-climbing

Jumping

and . . . flying.

On the first day of school Brer Rabbit combed his ears and went off to his running class. There he was a star. He ran to the top of the hill and back as fast as he could go, and oh, didn't it feel good.

The next class was swimming. When the rabbit smelt the chlorine he said, 'Wait a minute! Rabbits don't like to swim.'

The instructor said, 'Well you may not like it now, but five years from now you'll know it was a good thing for you.'

In the tree-climbing lesson a tree trunk was set at a 30 degree angle so all the animals had a chance to succeed. The little rabbit tried so hard he hurt his leg.

In the jumping lesson, the rabbit got along well. In the flying lesson, he had a problem. So the teacher gave him a psychological test and discovered he belonged in remedial flying.

The next morning he went on to his swimming

lesson. The instructor said, 'Today we jump into the water.'

'Wait, wait. I talked to my parents about swimming. They didn't learn to swim. We don't like to get wet. I'd like to stop this course.'

The instructor said, 'You can't stop it now. At this point you have a choice: either you jump in or you fail.'

The rabbit jumped in. He panicked! He went down once. He went down twice. Bubbles came up. The instructor saw that he was drowning and pulled him out. The other animals had never seen anything quite as funny as this wet rabbit who looked more like a rat without a tail, and so they chirped and jumped and barked and laughed at the rabbit. The rabbit was more humiliated than he had ever been in his life. He wanted desperately to get out of the lesson that day. He was glad when it was over.

He thought he would head for home, that his parents would understand and help him. When he arrived he said to his parents, 'I don't like school. I just want to be free.'

'If rabbits are going to get ahead, you have to get a diploma,' replied his parents.

The rabbit said, 'I don't want a diploma.'

The parents said, 'You're going to get a diploma whether you like it or not.'

They argued and finally the parents made the rabbit go to bed. In the morning the rabbit headed off for school with a slow hop. Then he remembered that the head teacher had said that any time he had a problem he should remember that the school counsellor's door is always open.

When he arrived at school he hopped up in the chair by the school counsellor and said, 'I don't like school.'

And the school counsellor said, 'Mmmm – tell me about it.'

And the rabbit did.

The school counsellor said, 'Rabbit, I hear you. I hear you say that you don't like school because you don't like swimming. I think I have diagnosed that correctly. Rabbit, I tell you what we'll do. You're doing well in running. I don't know why you need to work on running. I'll arrange it so you don't have to go running any more; you can have two periods of swimming instead.'

When the rabbit heard that he was very upset!

As the rabbit hopped out of the school counsellor's office he looked up and saw his friend the wise old owl, who cocked his head and said, 'Brer Rabbit, life doesn't have to be this way. We could have schools and businesses where people are allowed to concentrate on what they do well.'

Brer Rabbit was inspired. He thought that when he graduated, he would start a business where the rabbits would do nothing but run, the squirrels could just climb trees, and the fish could just swim. As he disappeared into the meadow, he sighed softly to himself and said, 'Oh my, what a great place that would be.'[23]

When we are allowed to use the special gifts that God has given us, life not only becomes more fulfilling but more effective. Other people's armour may look good but when we operate within our own gifting we find that giants fall faster.

I just wish I'd learnt it earlier.

My mother is ninety years old. Over almost a century she has accumulated many skills but she has mastered none so well as her ability as a gardener.

I have seen a small tree that was all but dead succumb to her care and, like a sick child who suddenly finds himself a patient in the finest hospital in the land, become strong again.

As I have watched her I have often thought of a phrase that Jesus used. He said, 'My Father is the gardener.' The phrase is pregnant with meaning. There are many levels at which it can be understood, but of this, at least, I am sure: that with this gardener great trees can grow from small beginnings, that sickly plants that have almost given up can find life again . . . and that in his garden there are sometimes a few surprises.

5

My Father is the gardener

When I was fifteen years old I wanted to be a rock and roll singer. I ended up as a senior partner in a law practice, and later as Executive Director of a national charity, but my heart then was in being able to master 'Johnny B. Goode' with three chords and a guitar that kept in tune worse than I did. Even now, sometimes, in the quiet of the early morning darkness, I consider all I am involved in and wonder if I would trade it all to walk onto the stage at Las Vegas and take my bow. Elvis was my hero. I had developed the art of lifting my top lip in that half sneer, half smile of his that I was convinced drove girls to distraction. I had an Elvis hairstyle, walked liked Elvis, talked like Elvis and sang like me.

And one day as I strode down my street humming 'Blue suede shoes' a man from our church approached me and asked if I'd like to do a Bible study once a week with him. He told me places were limited – apparently there were to be just two teenagers in his class. The boy whose life ambition was to climb into a gold lamé suit said, 'Yes.'

Some time, deep in eternity, I will discover why I said 'Yes' that day, but when I was fifteen years old – smoking, sneaking off to dances, and dreaming of stardom – I began a weekly Bible study.

He and his wife were poor but no poorer than us; like us they did not own a house or a car, they shared a bathroom with the people upstairs. He had no qualifications and an ordinary job at which he worked hard to make ends meet. The course that we studied together had not exactly been written for a boy who wanted to make it to Las Vegas, but I never missed an evening.

He was a brilliant psychologist. We would study the Bible for thirty minutes, and then he would produce two pieces of hardboard which he would lay across the dining table, and hey presto – table tennis! But never before had the game been played in such a fashion. The small makeshift table filled the room, and we would play our shots with our hands tight to our chests. If the ball went under the table it was a five minute job to retrieve it.

And after table tennis we would walk to the fish and chip shop together. By the time we got back the vinegar was seeping through the wrappings and his wife had the tea brewing. We loved those evenings. Don't tell me we loved them because in those far-off days teenagers were simple and easy to please. No, we went because this couple made us feel special. It was fun, and at times stretching, but not in a school way, and we felt as though we were somebody.

One night after a year of study he said to me, 'I want to see if you could learn to speak in public.' He took an old flannelgraph from a cupboard. For the uninitiated I should explain: it was a sheet of felt on which a scene had been printed – in this case of a hillside. The cardboard box that lay next to it contained all the equipment needed to tell the parable of the prodigal son – cut-outs of pigs, son, father and elder brother. The characters stuck to the felt and you put them on, or removed them, as you told the story.

It took months of practice. There were moments when it seemed certain that a career in public speaking was not likely; I remember one dark moment when I managed to get the old father in the sty and had a pig looking down the road waiting for his son to come home. But I got there eventually and one day he said to me, 'You're ready to take a children's meeting at church.'

Twenty years later I rang him from Vienna. The next day I was a keynote speaker, addressing a thousand lawyers at an International Law Conference. I said, 'You taught me to do it – it is because of you.' Since the start of Care for the Family I speak to him more often. I say to him, 'I've passed some of the skills you taught me on to others. Last night we spoke to thousands of people, or on this television programme or that radio station. We are reaching millions with a message that can revolutionize lives. You started it!'

So often we feel we have so little to offer. We look at society today, we perhaps mourn at the state of the church, we see men and women of great ability in prominent roles and say in our hearts, 'Thank goodness they are doing it – I have nothing to offer.' But that is always wrong. In fact it is almost sinful. It was Abraham Lincoln who said, 'God loves ordinary people – he made so many of them.' And the story of the Bible is of God using those who so often felt they had little to give to change the world. 'But God chose the foolish things of the world to shame the wise; God chose the weak things of the world to shame the strong. He chose the lowly things . . . so that no-one may boast before him.'[24]

I wonder how the young boy felt when the idea first crossed his mind. He had sat engrossed as the carpenter taught. Occasionally he would look around at the vast crowd sitting on the hillside over-looking Galilee. And then he realised something was wrong. He had seen James whisper something into the Teacher's ear and then look crestfallen at whatever reply he had received. He could see the disciples arguing amongst themselves. He heard one of them say, 'A year's pay would not feed all these.' So that was it. The people were hungry, the Teacher had told them to feed the crowd – but they had nothing.

And then the thought had risen in his heart. He began to get up, and practically fell again, his legs had all but gone to sleep. But soon he was pushing his way through the crowd, 'Excuse me, I have to get this to the Master.' And it was then he heard the voice in his heart, 'Who do you think you are? Sit down now before you embarrass yourself. That's Peter and John out there, do you think you know better than them? You're just a boy – forget your wild plans.'

He would have sat down that very moment – except he knew that if he did he would regret it even when he was an old man – and suddenly he was there, face to face with Andrew. 'It's just my lunch – my mother made it – a few fish and a little bread. If he wants it he can have it.'

He would never forget what he saw that day on the hillside at Galilee. The Master opened the cloth around his food and took out the bread, then the fish. He saw the hands of the carpenter hold them high above the crowd and call down the blessing of God. And then his lunch – the food his mother had prepared – was being broken to the crowd. When he was old he would tell the story to his grandchildren.[25]

Our church has a programme to help those who are homeless. Each week people bring food and clothing and, perhaps even more importantly, a sense of dignity to those that few others want to touch. Some years ago a mother in the church began to help. I have never heard her speak from the platform, she is often silent in house-group Bible studies, she has felt in the past she had little to give. The other night I discovered by accident that near to Christmas she had gone back into the city centre late one night to find a man she had noticed who had no buttons on his coat. She sat beneath an arch and she sewed buttons on the jacket of the man, who smelt and who was cold. I have no doubt that there were many things that she felt she could not do but a man's life was touched that night because she did what she could.

Some years ago I was speaking at a conference; I had been talking about the feeding of the five thousand, and in particular the young boy who gave his lunch away to the Master. I had urged each of us to discover something we could do for the Kingdom, no matter how small, and to do it with all our heart. A woman came up to me after the event and told me the story of her grand-daughter. The child was five years old and one day said to her mother,

'Mum, when is Jesus coming to our village?'

The mother was taken aback. 'Darling,' she said, 'he is always with us.'

The child replied, 'I know that, but when is he coming to our village?'

The mother pulled the child to her and asked, 'Why is this so important to you?'

'Well,' said the little girl, 'they have been telling me about him in Sunday School and all the things he did. I've saved my pocket money and I've got enough to buy five loaves of bread and two fish. If I could just get them to Jesus – he could feed the world.'

Don't spend your life wishing you could have done more – do today the small thing you can. And when you plant that seed you never know where it will end.

After all, your Father is the gardener.

All your strength is in your union.
All your danger is in discord.

Henry Wadsworth Longfellow, *Hiawatha*

To love at all is to be vulnerable. Love anything
and your heart will be wrung and possibly be
broken. If you want to make sure of keeping
it intact, you must give your heart to no-one,
not even an animal. Wrap it up carefully
around with hobbies and little luxuries; avoid
all entanglements; lock it up safe in the casket
or coffin of your selfishness . . . The only place
outside heaven where you can be perfectly safe
from all the dangers . . . of love is hell.[26]

C. S. Lewis, *The Four Loves*

6

I was meant to party with my enemies

Within twenty-four hours he would be dead and buried. It was probably a Thursday evening – Passover evening – and he had just a few hours left with his friends before those determined to kill him came for him. The room was prepared and now they could eat the sacred meal together.[27] And it was then, just as everything seemed ready, that it happened; the disciples realised there was no servant to wash their feet. Washing feet before dinner in the culture of the first century wasn't just tradition – it made for a sweeter atmosphere all around. But there was no one to do it. No one who would bend and wash away the dust and the dirt. They looked at one another for a while. In fairness things were pretty tense anyway; they had only just had an argument as to which of them was the greatest, so they weren't falling over themselves to do the servant's job.

And it was at that moment, as they were sitting petulantly, that they saw him rise from his seat, take a towel, and begin the task. James can remember what it felt like to have the Master rub away the dirt, and dry his feet. He felt ashamed and somehow humiliated, as if he should have known better. Peter took it worst of all. He never did anything by halves and simply refused to let Jesus wash his feet. But with tears and blushes the job was finally done.

They watched him take his seat again, and just knew that he was going to say something they would never forget, 'Now that I, your Lord and Teacher, have washed your feet, you should also wash one another's feet[28]. . . . As I have loved you, so you must love one another.'[29]

There must have been so many issues that he could have brought to their hearts and minds on that last night but he chose this one. *He wanted them to love each other*. For some reason best known to his eternal heart, this matters to God more than whether we build the church extension, use modern songs or the old green hymn book, sit sombrely in church or swing from the chandeliers, get to all the meetings, or have a fish badge on the back of our car.

He wants us to love each other.

Now here is a very strange thing. You can travel the length and breadth of this country and attend churches of all kinds. Your mind will be blown by the deadness of some and the life of others. You will experience beautiful liturgy, imaginative modern worship, and programmes enough to make you tired just listening to the notices. If you 'church-hop' you will at times believe that you have truly found the place 'just for you'. You say to friends, 'I know it's not perfect.' But in your heart you think it is. And that glorious state may last for a couple of years and then it will begin to dawn on you that never mind loving each other, some of the members actually hate each other.

You begin to hear murmurings of discontent. Classic comments are 'I only care for the good of this church,' or 'I have been here from the beginning.' (The speaker is not claiming eternal status, just that they were on the very first building committee.) You start to notice that annual church meetings have the flavour of cup-ties. It's true that the opposing teams do not actually wear different colours but they do sit together in the stadium and they do predictably roar their approval or boo according to how their team is doing.

And then you realise something that at first you find hard to believe: that although these people have a manifesto of things they want to change – the worship, the teaching, the leaders, the youth leader, or the piano – actually those issues are not at the core of the problem. If all those things were sorted out immediately they would at once move on to something else. No, the real issue is relationships. And it is a tragedy.

It is a tragedy because it may well be that when we get to heaven we will discover that it wasn't of eternal consequence whether we met in a mega-church or a fifty-seater chapel; that actually God enjoyed worship equally well sung from an overhead projector or a hymn book; and heaven was never really holding its breath over whether we would take out the old pulpit and put in a full lighting rig. But if we do not strive for unity in our churches it is impossible that we will not feel ashamed when we meet him. This matters to him.

Over the past few years I have been presenting a seminar series on the issue of stress management. As I have talked with people after the event, or read the 'hurt mail' that comes into our office, I have become more and more convinced that the lives many of us lead as Christians are in fact more stressful than those of people outside the church. Now this would be acceptable if the kind of stress we are facing came out of our stand for the faith. Jesus warned his followers that discipleship was anything but an easy option. The problem is that many of us don't get near that kind of stress because we are too busy with a different kind – the kind that the Christian community imposes on itself. The church itself is becoming the greatest stress factor in the lives of many who are members.

You may have heard of the vicar who was last to leave the church after a particularly difficult deacons' meeting. It was late and as he walked across the car park it was deserted save for his vehicle and an empty Coca-Cola can which he kicked with sheer frustration. As he did so a genie came out and explained that the kick had freed him and the vicar could have any wish he wanted. The genie explained, however, that he was only a junior genie and the wish ought not to be too difficult.

The vicar thought a moment: he had so many needs – finance at home, a new car, a roof that needed mending, to name but a few – but finally the selfless part of him rose to the top and he heard himself say, 'An end to all war and violence for ever.'

The genie looked stunned and said, 'I told you I was only a junior genie, could you try me with something easier?'

'Oh, very well,' said the vicar, 'could you make the people in the diaconate a little more amenable and not quite so difficult?'

The genie hesitated and said, 'Would you mind very much if we go back to your original wish?'

'People stress' is killing us; we are burning *each other* out. Rather than demonstrating the mutual support and encouragement we need if we are to reach a broken world, many of us are consumed with battles within the fellowship. You may say, 'But you don't know what difficult people we have in our church.' The truth is that we all have difficult people in our lives. You may think that in your church you have the most difficult person in the world, but you don't. There are difficult people in other churches that would make yours look like long-lost friends.

But difficult people need difficult issues to keep them going, and here again your church doesn't have the monopoly. A leading contender in this department is normally the music. This could be too loud, too modern or too ancient. Running a close second to the style of worship will be the teaching; this can be too deep, too shallow, or too long. Other issues will be the youth work, the building and, of course, the style of leadership.

It will be a great stress reliever if we can learn to live with our difficult people. A railway company once realised that it was always the last carriage on the train that was involved in accidents; so they decided to remove it. Difficult people in church life are like that. You dream of the day they will leave. One day they do and you look forward to a time of unsullied bliss. But almost as soon as their feet are out of the door others rise up to take their place. These new ones are more difficult than the old ones dreamt of being – seemingly trained by watching their predecessors. It is not always possible, but if we can we should try to live with the ones we've got; after all, in their eyes, we're probably difficult too.

However, the issue is deeper than this and there are some important considerations in local church life that we ignore at our peril.

The first of these is that the local church is not the playground. In the playground there are unwritten rules. The first of these is that you play with your friends. Church is not meant to be that way. Jesus gave a hint of it when he talked about not just inviting your friends to your parties. The world does that. You can have a room full of like-minded people having fun together in any old club in the world. But life in God's kingdom should be different; this kingdom is about enemies joining in, going 'extra miles' and the royal law of love. What it is not about is a group of like-minded people feeding each other's discontent. The urgency of getting this right comes over powerfully in the letter Paul wrote to the Christians at Corinth:

> I have a serious concern to bring up with you, my friends, using the authority of Jesus our Master. I'll put it as urgently as I can. You *must* get along with each other. You must learn to be considerate of one another, cultivating a life in common . . . You're fighting amongst yourselves . . . You're all picking sides, going around saying, 'I'm on Paul's side,' or 'I'm for Apollos,' or 'Peter is my man,' or 'I'm in the Messiah group.' I ask you, 'Has the Messiah been chopped up in little pieces so we can each have a relic all our own?'[30]

I have a hunch that when we stand before him we will find that God was not as concerned about the music, the building or even the style of teaching as we were. What he will want to know is how much we sweated, bled and struggled, what price we paid as peacemakers that the prayer of his son that 'they may be one'[31] might be fulfilled on earth.

And in the playground we have the wonderful sanction that if things don't work out as we want, we can always take our ball home. And in church if we are upset then we can stop giving financially, or threaten some other sanction, but we would do well to remember that is not how God normally deals with us. If God withdrew his favour from us the second we cease to please him we would find that our very next breath

71

is in danger. Our money and our gifts are not ours to barter with – they belong to him.

We may decide to leave the church, and I fully understand that some do it after years of heart-searching and honestly believing there is no alternative; it may be that sometimes there is no other way, but it is a massive step. I am staggered at the speed at which some people move from church to church because they are unhappy. You rarely find they have moved because they suspect heresy; it is far more likely that this new church doesn't suit them any longer. Once embarked upon, it is a weary road they have chosen for they are destined to *never* find their perfect church and to drive others to despair trying to please them.

And in the playground there is little forgiveness. You can lose your status as 'best friend' by offering the bag of sweets to the wrong person. But church should be different. It is not a surprise to God that Christians have such a hard time getting on with each other. That is the very reason why the ministry of Jesus and the letters of the New Testament are continually talking about putting things right with people, forgetting the past, not nursing our hurts – in short, about forgiveness. When we cannot or will not strive for forgiveness, we become bitter. Forgiveness is at the heart of God's kingdom. This is not a matter of having all our hurts sorted out so that we feel good about them; it is rather the principle of letting go of them, remembering that they are nothing compared to the hurt we bring to God.

It's time to be honest. We are all difficult in some

way. We can all be bruised or offended and each of us has an inalienable belief in our own 'rightness'. But if we do not strive to be peacemakers it is not different music we need, or a better youth leader, or a new building or even deeper teaching. Our need is for God to reveal to us how much we owe to him. This is not a matter of agreeing with each other, or going on holiday with people we can't stand. It's about striving, bleeding for unity. It's about laying down agendas that don't matter, letting go of personal hurts and ambitions, denying ourselves the warm satisfaction of gossip, and growing up spiritually.

The local church is an awesome invention. It is not a mistake in the mind of God. When a church cares more about what matters to God than anything else, there is no end to what it can achieve – no matter what its type, style or denomination. We are a special people on a special mission and when we bring each other down we make it hard for us to be effective.

That's why James says:

Don't bad-mouth each other, friends. It's God's Word, his Message, his Royal Rule, that takes a beating in that kind of talk. You're supposed to be honouring the Message, not writing graffiti all over it.[32]

We live in a broken world that is crying out for help. People have an ever-increasing belief that they are worthless; we have a growing sense of meaninglessness in society today and many experience poverty that shames us all. There are single parents to sustain, lonely people to comfort, families that are breaking up so fast it's taking our breath away, and, above all, there are people, ordinary people, who need somebody to tell them about Christ. We simply do not have time to major on minors; the task is too great and too urgent.

I'm old enough to remember the cod war. I should say that the name was deceptive. Never in the history of fishing have cod been so safe. And the reason was that the cod war was actually between the fishermen. They cut each other's nets and generally made life as difficult as possible for each other. In fact, if you were a cod it was time to get your Lilo out and enjoy the sun. Do we really think that those outside the church care about our petty squabbles, and does it no longer hurt us that God's name is tarnished by our divisions? Why have we found it so hard to believe that loving each other matters to God?

Walking one night

Walking through the city late one night, I came upon a guy about to jump off a skyscraper. I said, 'Wait a minute, don't you believe in God?'

He said, 'I do believe in God.'

I said, 'Really? Are you a Christian or a Jew?'

He said, 'I'm a Christian.'

I said, 'Me too!' I said, 'Are you a Protestant or a Catholic?'

He said, 'A Protestant.'

I said, 'Really, what denomination?'

He said, 'Baptist.'

I said, 'Me too. Northern or Southern?'

He said, 'Northern.'

I said, 'Northern Conservative Baptist or Northern Liberal Baptist?'

He said, 'Northern Conservative Baptist.'

I said, 'Me too! Northern Conservative Reformed Baptist or Northern Conservative Fundamentalist Baptist?'

He said, 'Northern Conservative Fundamentalist Baptist.'

I said, 'Me too! Northern Conservative Fundamentalist Baptist Great Lakes Region or Northern Conservative Fundamentalist Baptist Eastern Region?'

He said, 'Northern Conservative Fundamentalist Baptist Great Lakes Region.'

I said, 'Me too! This is incredible! Northern Conservative Fundamentalist Baptist Great Lakes Region Council of 1879 or Northern Conservative Fundamentalist Baptist Great Lakes Region Council of 1912?'

He said, 'Northern Conservative Fundamentalist Baptist Great Lakes Region Council of 1912.'

I said, 'Die, heretic!' and pushed him off. [33]

Last Sunday in a church somewhere near you, somebody

was hurt. Even if that organisation has a super-efficient church administrator who logs every injury on church premises in an accident book, the page for that day will be blank. And yet, in spite of the fact that no record exists of this event, the repercussions of it will affect that church for the next decade. Because of this event there will be small children who never get to hear of the Sunday School, let alone attend it. Because this thing occurred, there will be broken families that never get help, and others for whom the message of the faith remains a mystery – shrouded in the fog of the church that stands in the heart of their neighbourhood.

It is true that the act did not seem significant at the time but it contained a seed that nobody saw hit the ground that day. Over the coming months and years that seed will grow in secret like a cancer and finally pick its moment. When its fruit blossoms the poison it contains will explode with devastating effect. Years later people will ask, 'What happened to that congregation?', but nobody will remember the event through which it all began – an act that eventually paralysed that church, then split it, and finally, as hell laughed loudly, spewed it out all over the neighbourhood.

Well, what is this great event that happened last week in a church near you (perhaps *very* near)? I have painted the outcome of it in such cataclysmic terms that now, when I mention it, you won't believe me. But it is true: last Sunday somebody was offended, their feelings were hurt, they felt slighted in some way. It almost certainly wasn't as important as doctrine and perhaps it was something relatively insignificant. It just may have touched somebody in the area of their self-worth or ego; it was important to them.

The Bible assumes it will happen; when it comes to life in the local church it presupposes that we will hurt each other, disagree, fall out, and for that very reason whole chunks of it are dedicated to facing the person who has hurt us, telling them they have done so, forgiving, striving for peace, letting go of our petty hurts, and all for the utterly compelling reason that God has forgiven us.

But it is here that we meet a very great difficulty; it is a matter of great sadness. It is simply that many of us live in two worlds. In one of these worlds – our 'church world' – there are sermons. Those talks are full of teaching on forgiveness, grace, love and what it means to suffer for Jesus' sake. In that world, as well as sermons, there is what we call Christian service. This could be youth work, music, missions, projects for disabled people or house-group leadership. This is what we 'do'. And there are books in that world – books on holiness, prayer, tithing, forgiveness and church planting.

But there is always, alongside that world, another place. This is our 'inner world'. This is the part of us from which we run our lives. We were not aware of doing so but long ago we erected vast Chinese walls between the two worlds. If somebody preaches on giving sacrificially in the 'church world' we agree with them, but later when we look at our bank statement in the 'inner world' we find that it is untouched by any recent debit. We sing in the 'church world' of our desire to tell the world the message of the King, but when we glance into the 'inner world' we discover that our next-door neighbours have never been invited in for coffee.

And in the 'church world' we thank God that he has forgiven us, time and time again. In this world we acknowledge that very forgiveness as our only hope in eternity – that when we hurt him deeply our relationship can be restored. But the hurt last week will occur in the 'inner world', in that part of our being which is untouched by the Spirit of God and his gentleness. And so we will deal with it as would anybody else. We will nurse it, and soon we will find others who themselves have been hurt by that person and we will share our experiences. And the bitterness and the anger and the hate will grow so that it is quite out of proportion to the original hurt. And one day we will get revenge. Oh, such a moment will be dressed up in religious language, but it will be common or garden hell at work.

And all would be well were it not for two things: the first is that God is the reader of men and women's hearts and can therefore look over walls; the second is that we will meet him. The day will come faster than we think. Death will say, 'Now' and we will stand before him. We will not be proud in that day over some of the battles that seem so vital now. And so while there is still time, let us lay down every personal agenda, let us be willing to 'spend and be spent' for the sake of the kingdom, so that in that moment we will not be ashamed. And so a broken world can again look to its local church with hope.

The parable of the geese

Next autumn, when you see the geese heading south for the winter, flying along in a V-shaped formation, you might consider what science has discovered as to why they fly that way. As each bird flaps its wings it creates an uplift for the bird immediately following. By flying in a V-formation the whole flock adds at least 70% more to its flying range than if each bird were flying in its own.

When a goose falls out of formation it suddenly feels the drag and resistance of trying to go it alone, and quickly gets back into formation to take advantage of the lifting power of the bird in front.

When the leading goose gets tired it rotates back in the wing and another goose flies point. It is sensible to take turns doing demanding jobs . . . whether with people or with geese flying south. Geese honk from behind to encourage those up front to keep up their speed.

When a goose gets sick, or is wounded by gunshot and falls out of formation, one or two of the other geese fall out with it and follow it down to lend help and protection. They stay with the fallen goose until it is able to fly or until it dies.

Only then do they launch out on their own, or with another formation, to catch up with their group.

People who share a common direction and sense of community can get where they are going much more quickly and easily because they are travelling on the thrust of one another's efforts. If we have as much sense as a goose we will stay in formation with those who are headed the same way we are. If we have the sense of a goose, we will stand by each other when danger threatens or trouble comes.[34]

A prayer of Jesus shortly before he died:

Father, the time has come. Glorify your Son, that your Son may glorify you . . . I have revealed you to those whom you gave me . . . I will remain in the world no longer, but they are still in the world, and I am coming to you. Holy Father, protect them by the power of your name – the name you gave me – so that they may be one as we are one . . . My prayer is not for them alone. I pray also for those who will believe in me through their message, that all of them may be one . . . that the world may believe that you have sent me.[35]

If you want to live a radical Christian life that will catch the attention of those who have no faith; if you want to belong to a church that, no matter how large or small, will be a revolutionary force for good, there is a way it can be achieved, but do not turn first to systems, meetings, or even church growth strategies: instead, party with your enemies.

I wish I had learnt it a lot earlier.

On the Mount of Crucifixion
Fountains opened deep and wide
Through the floodgates of God's mercy
Flowed a vast and gracious tide.
Grace and love, like mighty rivers,
Poured incessant from above.
And heaven's peace and perfect justice
Kissed a guilty world in love.

If you told me that for the rest of my life I could
only live in the good of <u>one</u> of my lessons it
would be the one that follows.

7

The kiss of God

The place was Enniskillen in Northern Ireland. As a
crowd of people were honouring those who had died in
two world wars the bomb went off. Gordon Wilson held
his daughter, Marie, in his arms as she died. The next
day a single word was being telephoned, faxed, copied
around the news agencies of the world. That single
word became the headline of newspapers across the
United Kingdom – the man was interviewed on national
television. Such was its impact that the Queen referred
to it in her Christmas broadcast that year; the word
was 'forgiveness'. Gordon Wilson said that he forgave
those who had killed his child. Not everybody agreed
– there were not a few who said that to forgive like
that was wrong – but whatever you believed, there was
no doubt that we were witnessing something unusual,
something almost from another world. Some said –
almost Godlike.

Just recently I shared with a close friend a situation
I felt I had handled badly. I had put it right as far as

I could, but it still weighed heavily on me. When we finished talking I asked him to pray for me. I can't remember all of his prayer but one short phrase touched my heart. He said, 'Lord you have forgiven him. Help him to let go of it; *it's in the past.*'

'In the past' – just a common phrase and yet in those circumstances full of power. What my friend meant when he prayed with me that day is that ultimately what I did wrong I did against God and he has forgiven me. We sometimes hear people say, 'Oh, I have forgiven him but things can never be the same between us again.' But that is not how God forgives. Imagine you are a child again; you have hurt your father. He deals with you sternly and then, seeing your tears and knowing how sorry you are, he draws you to him. You cannot stop crying and you see his brow furrow as he searches for a way to tell you it is all right between you now. Then suddenly he leaves the room, but he is only gone a moment and when he returns he has in his hand a globe of the world. And then he kneels, looks you in the eye and says, 'Do you know how far the East is from the West – see here is the West . . .' Then his finger slowly moves around the circumference of the earth: you pass cities, countries, oceans, continents. Finally his finger stops, '. . . and here is the East. That is how far away I have put in my mind and heart what you did.[36] It is in the past; you and I must forget it now.'

One of the most powerful illustrations of that situation occurs in Dr Luke's record of the life of Christ.[37] Jesus is at a party held by a religious leader. In those days it was common courtesy to wash the feet of the guests, to give a kiss of welcome, and put a little oil on the head. Simon the Pharisee does none of these for the young teacher – it was a calculated insult. Somehow a woman, probably a prostitute, gets into the party. She is somebody whose life has been changed by Jesus and she begins to put right the insults to the man who had revolutionised her life. When the host sees this, he says to himself, 'This man is no prophet – if he was, he would know who she is and he wouldn't let her touch him.'

And it was at that moment that Jesus told his host a story. It concerned two men who owed sums to a money-lender. One owed a great deal of money and the other a much smaller amount. Neither could pay and the money-lender forgave them both the debt. When he had finished the story Jesus turned to his host, 'Now Simon, which of them will love him more?' The Pharisee was not a stupid man. 'I suppose the one who had the bigger debt cancelled.' 'You have judged correctly,' Jesus said.

When he looked back on what occurred next, Simon couldn't quite remember how it had all happened. One moment he was answering an irritating question from the young carpenter, the next he was reeling as he realised this man was reading his very thoughts. 'Simon, do you see this woman? When I came into your house you did not give me any water for my feet, but she wet them with her tears and dried them with her hair. You did not kiss me, but she has not stopped kissing my feet. You did not put oil on my head but she has poured perfume on my feet. And Simon, she loves much, because she has been forgiven much. *But he who has been forgiven little loves little.*'

And then he turned to the woman and said words to her that nobody who heard them that day ever forgot. Simon remembered until he died the uproar they caused in his party; the guests remembered screaming at the carpenter, 'Only God can say those words!' And every time the woman passed that familiar street corner, or saw a man's face that reminded her of the past, the words came back to her. He said, '*I forgive you.*'

I once saw a circus elephant tethered to a post with a thin piece of string. With a flick of its leg, it could have easily torn the string and post from the ground but it didn't. And that is because when the animal was young, the rope was attached to a chain which was wrapped around a post sunk deep into the ground. The young elephant tried hard to get free, but the rope never gave and it bit into him with every pull. And then one day the trainer removed the rope and chain and tied the elephant with string attached to a small stake in the ground. The elephant looked at it; it seemed so fragile. But then old memories came flooding back. He believed that if he pulled the string, the pain would come. He decided he could not be free, and he would never try again.

Many of us live our lives tethered to the past, but Christ has died for us and we should be free. When we accept forgiveness through his death the ancient hold is broken. To live tied to the past is to live in a prison; it is to live carrying a weight on one's back; it is to sit like a bird in a cage gazing at blue skies through an *open* door.

In *The Pilgrim's Progress* John Bunyan put it like this:

> He ran thus till he came at a place somewhat ascending, and upon that place stood a Cross, and a little below, in the bottom, a Sepulchre. So I saw in my dream, that just as Christian came up with the Cross, his burden loosed from off his shoulders, and fell from off his back; and began to tumble. And continued to do, till it came to the mouth of the Sepulchre, where it fell in, and I saw it no more.[38]

The parable of the prodigal son[39] has been called 'the greatest short story ever written'. It is captivating in so many ways but, for me, the heart of it is the surprise. The boy gets to a stage where he knows he has made a dreadful mistake. The Jewish audience must have recoiled in horror as Jesus told how the son ended up in a pig-sty. And he decides to make for home, but not as a son – he believes his days as a son are gone. He decides to ask for a job as a servant, and prepares a speech along those lines in preparation for the day he'll meet his father again.

What he doesn't know is that every evening since he left home, the old man has climbed onto the flat roof of the house and strained his eyes down the road to look for his boy. And when, one day, he sees him, he runs. The account has little sophistication in it – the old man is running and then falling on his son's neck and kissing him. The boy begins his speech, 'Father I am no more worthy to be called your son . . .,' but he never finishes it. The old man shouts, 'Put a ring on his finger, shoes on his feet and start the celebrations; my son is home again.'

You may know times like that in your walk with God. You will sit covered in shame in some pig-sty somewhere and believe there is no way back. But he waits for you. You must be sorry for the past, you must want more than anything else to walk a different way in the future, but you must also remember you are his son, his daughter, and you should begin the long walk home.

Such forgiveness is hard to grasp. We live in a world where we are used to earning things – money, position, reputation. We have phrases like, 'Now you've proved yourself you can have more responsibility.' Much of that is not wrong, but the only thing you bring to the cross of Jesus is the wrong you have done; you cannot earn this forgiveness; this above all is free.

We can miss this forgiveness for other reasons: the great hope for the boy in the parable lay in the fact that he knew he was in a pig-sty and far from the father's house. But it is possible to become self-righteous, to have lost a sensitivity to the Spirit of God, and therefore an understanding of our real condition. Somebody put it like this: 'Our churches are full of nice, kind, loving people who have never known the despair of guilt or the breathless wonder of forgiveness.' As I was thinking about this concept some years ago, I had a picture of Jesus stalking down the corridor of a prison; on the doors were written the crimes that had been committed but he was flinging open prison doors and shouting, 'You can be forgiven!' And then the picture changed. The prison corridor was still there and he still stalked down it, but this time on the doors were written wrongs that policemen do not catch you for – greed and arrogance, pride and gossip, lack of love and a disregard of the weak; but to those, too, he shouted, 'You can be forgiven.'

But perhaps above all, we miss this forgiveness because we will not forgive those who wrong us. The words of Jesus could not be clearer, 'If you do not forgive those who hurt you, neither will your heavenly father forgive you.' At the heart of the Lord's Prayer is the plea, 'Forgive us our sins, for we also forgive everyone who sins against us.'[40]

There was a man who owed a king a great deal of money and, when he could not pay, the king forgave him. That man then went out and found a man who owed him just a few pounds and, when he could not pay, had him thrown into prison. When the king heard of it he was angry and had the first man brought to him and said, 'I forgave you much, should you not also have forgiven?' And he turned him over to the jailers.[41]

To forgive others can be very hard. I remember realising

very clearly that I had not forgiven somebody who had once hurt me badly. I had said I had forgiven him but I noticed that when others criticised him, I enjoyed it and caught myself saying, 'Me too – that's how he dealt with me as well.' I caught myself occasionally repeating to others the story of how he had hurt me, and discovered that rather than letting go of it I was, in fact, nursing it. It was *growing inside me.* That day I made a vow; it had several elements to it. Firstly, I would never again raise the matter with anybody. Secondly, I would, whenever possible, try to speak well of this person. Thirdly, I would not join in critical gossip about him. Fourthly, I would, so far as he would allow, try to rebuild the relationship. Fifthly, I would pray God's blessing on that man. As the years went by I felt my attitude to him soften and, perhaps, his did to me, for we were finally reconciled.

When we forgive it is not just for the sake of others. Often it is also *for our sake.* Dr R. T. Kendall of Westminster Chapel describes an occasion in which he had been badly hurt.

It was at the time of my greatest trial and the result was my self-justifying feeling of resentment, bitterness and self-pity. I could talk to nobody about it except my wife. During this time an old friend, Josif Tson of Romania, was passing through London and asked to see me. Little did I know this brief meeting was to be life-changing.

Since he was from outside London (and nobody

would know) I told him what they did to me. I poured my heart out and told him all I could think of. 'Is there anything more?' he asked. 'No, that's it,' I said.

Josif asked for fifteen minutes to take a brief nap and hoped I'd have a cup of tea ready for him. When he returned he took a sip of tea, then he pointed a finger at me. 'RT,' he began firmly in his lovely Romanian accent, 'You must totally forgive them. Until you totally forgive them, *you will be in chains*. Release them and you will be released.'

I said, 'Josif, I just remembered something else they did that I haven't told you.' But he was not interested in more of my self-pity. 'RT, you must totally forgive them. Release them and you will be released.'

It was my biggest test – the hardest thing I have ever had to do. But Josif was right – I was in chains and when I released them, I was free.

Sometimes this releasing of others is a gradual process. We wish that we could do it immediately but sometimes it is a build-up of small victories. We believe we have let them go but then suddenly the memory of the hurt comes flooding back and we feel the old bitterness rising in our hearts. It is then we need to release them afresh, and begin again. Such forgiveness is always hard, for sometimes as you cry 'forgive them' they are still banging nails into your hands and feet.[42] But it is our only hope of freedom, of being loosed from the chains of bitterness.

There may be occasions when we have to forgive those who don't even know they have wronged us. We felt the hurt deeply but if we went to them and said, 'I forgive you for what you did,' they wouldn't know what we were talking about. In these cases it is often best to say nothing; simply release them.

Sometimes it is hard to forgive because those who have wronged us show no regret; it seems at times that, given the chance, they would do it all again. In these circumstances it is very important to understand what forgiveness is not. It is not saying to them, 'What you did doesn't matter.' When Gordon Wilson in Enniskillen said he forgave those who had killed his daughter, he was not releasing them from the fact they will have to answer to God. He did not have the authority to do that.

We live in a moral universe in which men and women, unless they themselves have sought his forgiveness, will one day account for their actions before God. One of the most poignant newspaper cartoons of the last world war was set in a concentration camp. A line of Jewish people were being mown down by a storm trooper with a machine gun. Behind the soldier was a colonel who had a notebook and pencil and who was making a list of names and dates as the victims fell. But the soldier's face was half turned to a figure in white who stood behind the colonel. The colonel could not see him, but in the angel's hand was a notebook and a pencil, and he was recording . . . names and dates.

We know almost nothing about the man we meet in the Gospel accounts on the day that Jesus died. We are told he was a thief, and it was for that reason he was pinned with nails to a cross next to the young carpenter. We know that, whatever wrong he had done in his life, with his dying breath he sprang to the defence of the man the whole world seemed to want to kill. And we know that he yelled out, 'Jesus, remember me!'[43] And it was then that Jesus said something to him that has brought freedom and hope to millions of people down the generations and will go on doing so. He said, 'Today you will be with me in paradise.'[44] 'Today', 'with me', 'in paradise' – a Persian phrase that meant 'the garden of God'. But better than all of that was the implication that said to him, 'Everything that holds you to that cross I forgive. You are pinned with nails but – for the first time in your life – you are free.'

> On the Mount of Crucifixion
> Fountains opened deep and wide;
> Through the floodgates of God's mercy
> Flowed a vast and gracious tide.
> Grace and love, like mighty rivers,
> Poured incessant from above,
> And heaven's peace and perfect justice
> Kissed a guilty world in love.[45]

There is no message in the world like this: it can set you free and, if you live in the good of it, keep you free.

It is the kiss of God.

She sat in my study as I read her the draft of the next lesson. She is a friend, a colleague and one of the most gifted women I know. But she has known a lifetime of sickness. In her younger years she experienced depression that at times seemed to plunge her into a living hell. In more recent years she has had innumerable operations and on several occasions her life has hung in the balance. She is courageous beyond words and tells me it has not just been the excruciating pain that has brought her so low but the sheer frustration of having so much that she wants to do and yet spending much of her life feeling so very ill.

As I read this lesson to her she began to cry; first she sobbed quietly so that I was able to continue but then as I finished she cried uncontrollably. When she had composed herself she said, 'The love and support given to me by close friends and family over the years has been sent from heaven itself, but I have also spent a lifetime listening to Christians giving me answers as to why I have suffered. Some have said, "You must have offended God in some way." Others have offered, "If you had enough faith you could be well today." Some, trying to be kind, have suggested that God is trying to teach me something and I will be a better person because of my illness.'

And then she paused, and said through her tears, 'What they don't understand is that answers are not always vital to those who suffer. I don't always have to know why. There are comforts deeper than explanations.'

8

Sometimes answers aren't the last word

It was late on a cold February afternoon when I first walked alongside the railway track and under the arch that leads into the former concentration camp of Auschwitz. Less than sixty years ago that track carried cattle trucks with their cargoes of human life from all over Germany, Poland and France.

Those who came under the arch at Auschwitz had already suffered more than almost any man or woman can bear; many had travelled hundreds of miles with little water, no food and sharing the trucks with the corpses of loved ones who had died on the journey. It is difficult for us now, with the advantage of history, to believe that those people felt any sense of relief as they reached what we now call death camps, but they did. At last the journey was over, they had arrived, the future had to be better than the past. What more could their persecutors do to them?

The platform at which the trains used to stop is still there. To the right of the platform those that were fit and strong disembarked but those that were old or sick and the very young got off the train on the other side. And on the left, at the end of the platform, were the buildings. They were told they were showers and were hustled towards them. As they went in soap was given out. To the right of the buildings was the crematorium.

As the war was coming to an end and just before the Russian army entered Auschwitz the commandant ordered that the buildings at the end of the platform be blown up, but they never quite managed it. And on that cold day, with the mist coming in across the camp, I stood in the remains of the gas chambers. As I tried to picture the memories the walls held, I imagined I could hear the screams of those who first sensed that it was gas and not water pouring down on them. I bent and picked up a piece of stone, something to remind me of the moment. But then, as I gazed down at the piece of brick in my hand, I let it fall. To take it seemed sacrilege; this was not a time for souvenirs, the suffering was too great. In my heart I searched for answers to the question 'Why?' But I was strangely comforted by the fact that none came.

Sometimes answers come too quickly, for there are moments in life when we should accept that we do not understand. Times when we observe the deep suffering of others may well come into that category. On 13 March 1996, just before 9.30 in the morning, a gunman walked into the gymnasium of a primary school in Dunblane, Scotland and opened fire on the children and their teacher. Sixteen children and their teacher died that day; another twelve children and two teachers were injured.

Steve Chalke, who is both a Baptist minister and a television presenter, got a call from GMTV to fly to Dunblane to report on the situation. He was teamed up with Lorraine Kelly to co-present the bulletins. When he got there the cameras were already set up, but it was now dark and the temperature below freezing. He said that he and Lorraine stood frozen to the core, their hands so cold they could hardly hold the microphones. They would bring a short report and then, the second they were off air, dive into a car which had been left with the engine running and heater at full blast, to try to thaw out before the next report.

Steve and Lorraine were in the front seats and the cameramen in the back. The radio was on and the announcer introduced a member of the clergy who was asked to comment on why God allowed such suffering. Steve says that the man gave a good, robust, text-book answer, but with little compassion, anguish or pain. After he had finished there was a long silence in the car. Finally, one of the cameramen, almost in tears, stretched over, turned the radio off and said, 'Crap.' Steve said, 'I didn't disagree with the cleric's answer – everything he said had been entirely correct. It had just come at the wrong time, in the wrong place and in the wrong way.'

Just then it was time to go outside and back on air. As the red light flicked on the camera to show that people all over the country were now watching, Lorraine Kelly turned to Steve and said, 'Steve, people are blaming God for what has happened, what do you say to that?' Steve paused and then millions of people heard him say, 'That's all right; his shoulders are big enough.'

When Steve first told me what he had said my reaction was strange and I couldn't quite understand it. He had not defended God, he had not given any answers; he could easily have been misinterpreted and yet it seemed to me that his answer not only honoured those who were suffering, but God himself. It was as if God was sharing their suffering; he was part of it.

I have discovered that very often those who are going through deep suffering do not always want answers. They want to know that if there is a God in heaven, he understands their pain. Those of us who have become familiar with the Gospel accounts have a great difficulty in this area. We have become numb to the suffering he knew.

Today all over the world men and women will be tortured. As you read this, somebody is crying out in pain. Somewhere the modern equivalent of a crown of thorns is being forced on to a man's head. Somewhere, in a stinking cell, the words of Matthew's Gospel are being replayed today, 'They . . . took the staff and struck him on the head again and again.'[46]

And somewhere in our world today a woman is being betrayed by those she trusted. It may be a betrayal that will lead her to the executioner, as it did for him, or, more likely, it will be first noticed by the hotel receipt and the letter found in her husband's pocket as she searches for some keys. And I wonder, as she cries out in her pain, whether anybody will tell her that God understands betrayal.

And today there is somebody who, when it comes to the moment of greatest need, will be left alone by his friends. Oh, they will say kind things and promise to call, but as he walks away from them he will know in his heart that he is, in truth, utterly alone. It was so when God walked the earth. It was not even the pain of Peter's denial, which came as no surprise, but rather the inevitability that finally they would all leave him. All the promises, all the affection, all the bravado, would come to nothing.

And then there is that agonising cry from the cross, 'My God, my God, why have you forsaken me?'[47] I have heard preachers trying to explain away that God-forsaken cry. But it cannot be explained away. It is mysterious, it is filled with pain, it does not easily succumb to answers.

I was once involved in a debate on the subject of 'Why does God allow suffering?' Halfway through, it was interrupted by a man in a wheelchair. He had cerebral palsy. He could not keep his head still, saliva ran down his chin, but he gestured that he wanted to say something. His speech was hard to decipher, and it took him a long time to communicate what was on his heart, but it was simple and he repeated it for us, 'People look at me and say, "Why?" I look up at heaven and say, "Why not?"' The debate all but ground to a halt. We were now puzzled by a new phenomenon. It is that,

so often, those at the heart of the suffering are not asking
'Why?'

We need to walk humbly in this area. It is no shame
to say, 'I don't really understand why your pain is so
great, and why you, who are loving, have been so hurt.'
But we can then add, 'God understands your pain and he
is with you in it.' To those of us involved in the answers
business, in having everything wrapped up and labelled,
that doesn't seem much of a reply, but to those in the
deepest pain it often brings both comfort and hope.

In one of the oldest books in the Bible, Job searches
for answers to suffering; he looks up to heaven and asks,
'Why?' In one of the most dramatic renderings in the
whole of literature God answers him.

Who is this that darkens my counsel with words
without knowledge?
Brace yourself like a man and I will question
you,
and you shall answer me.

Where were you when I laid the earth's
foundations?
Tell me if you understand.
Who marked off its dimensions? Surely
you know.
On what were its footings set or who laid its
cornerstone?

Who shut up the sea behind doors when it burst
forth from the womb

when I said 'this is where your proud waves halt'?

Have you ever given orders to the morning or shown the dawn its place?
Have you journeyed into the springs of the sea or walked in the recesses of the deep?
Have the gates of death been shown to you?
Tell me, if you know all this.

Where does the light live?
And where does the darkness reside?
Do you know the path to their dwellings?
Surely you know, for you were already born
You have lived so many years!

Can you bind the beautiful Pleiades?
Can you loose the cords of Orion?
Do you hunt the prey for the lioness?
Do you give the horse its strength?
Does the hawk take flight by your wisdom?
Does the eagle soar at your command and build his nest on high?

The Lord said to Job, 'Let him who accuses God answer him.'

Then Job said, 'I put my hand over my mouth; I've said enough.'[48]

There have been moments in my life when I have sat by a hospital bed and cried with those who suffer. I have stood by graves that claimed lives far too young, and at times I have wept for my own pain. If at such times there are 'why's' that I can comprehend then whisper them to me. But you must also understand that at such moments reasons will not be my deepest need. And if in silence you simply hold me and cry with me, I *will* be comforted.

Death be not proud though some have
  called thee
Mighty and dreadful, for, thou art not so,
For, those, whom thou think'st thou dost
  overthrow,
Die not, poor death, nor yet canst thou
  kill me . . .
One short sleep past, we wake eternally,
And death shall be no more; *death thou
  shalt die.*

John Donne, *Death*

9

Death will die

There is, tucked away at the heart of the Hebrew Old Testament, a fascinating book. Its name has been interpreted in several ways – 'teacher', 'professor' – but I like best 'philosopher'. I choose that particular word because the book of Ecclesiastes is always asking the question 'Why?' It pushes us to consider the big questions of life and time and time again it does so by reminding us of the thing we do not want to hear: one day we will die.

In the early chapters of Ecclesiastes is a poem; the last line has in it the two great events of international life, 'A time for war and a time for peace,'[49] but the opening line has the two certainties of individual life, 'A time to be born and a time to die.'[50]

We don't like to talk about it; Os Guinness has called it 'the new pornography'. A hundred years ago it was sex that was taboo, but now in the number one slot is death. Some years ago I was at a party when the guests began to chat about their respective occupations.

I noticed that one woman was very reticent. Later, when the other guests had moved away, she whispered in my ear, 'I'm an undertaker.' She had learned over the years that the phrase was, in every sense, a party stopper.

We live with death and see more of it, second-hand, than any other society that has ever existed. Every news bulletin brings us pictures of it – train crashes, air disasters, wars and famine. And yet, unlike previous generations, many of us are quite old ourselves before we actually see a dead person. I wonder if it is that which allows many of us to go through life juggling two ideas: the first is that intellectually we know we are going to die; the second whispers to us, 'Not you.'

Of course whole industries have arisen to help us beat the odds. I am convinced that the battle against ageing is actually a battle against death. We do not want to grow old because we do not want to die. We do not wear the marks of age with pride as have other cultures; to us the wrinkles and the grey are a shame – a whisper of mortality. And so we can purchase 'ageing cream'. One poor man, untutored in the exact nature of this remedy, remarked to a friend who had been using it for months but whose face was still severely lined, 'Well, it seems to be working.'

But modern society is normally a little more sophisticated than that when it comes to pretending we can halt the march of time. When we are shown pictures of ageing actresses lounging across the centrefolds of magazines we do not give the game away, we do not talk of cosmetic surgery or make-overs or even old-fashioned corsets.

No, we smile in admiration and say, 'She's good . . . for her age.'

The battle reaches its intensity when we have to declare our true age. The idea that women hate doing this more than men is a nonsense. I remember being with a company director who I knew was fifty-six years old. When asked how old he was he replied, 'Middle-aged.' He got away with it but a colleague leant over to him and whispered in his ear, 'Middle-aged? How many people do you know of a hundred-and-twelve?'

There comes a time when we do not want to get old. I think it occurs at twenty-two. Until then we tend to add time on. I was at a friend's house recently; they have two children. When asked his age, Simon told me he was five-and-a-half, whereas Emma declared proudly she was eleven-and-three-quarters. Those fractions matter to them. But when we hit twenty-two we say, 'Just gone twenty.' Bob Hope was once interviewing an actress who, he sensed, wasn't quite as young as she made out. He said, 'Do you mind my asking how old you are?' She replied, 'Approaching forty.' Hope asked, 'From which direction?'

But it is all so understandable – the ageing process can be difficult to come to terms with. I read the other day that on your twenty-fifth school reunion you wear a badge so that others will know who you are; on your fiftieth school reunion you wear a badge so *you* will know who you are!

It is very hard, and yet time and time again the Bible urges us to be real about the fact that we are going to die. We can so easily believe that we have such power; we can put a man or woman on the moon, we can move information at frightening speeds, we can give a person a new heart, and yet what the old Jewish wise man said thousands of years ago is still true today, 'The length of our days is seventy years – or eighty, if we have the strength.'[51] And we are urged to 'number our days'.[52] That doesn't mean we can guarantee how long we have left to live. When he was diagnosed with cancer, the entertainer Roy Castle was asked by a reporter, 'What's it like to have only three months to live?'

'Well,' said Roy, 'it's not so bad – *you* can't even guarantee you've got tomorrow!'

The principle of numbering our days means we acknowledge the brevity of this life. It urges us not to get too preoccupied with buildings or money or prestige because those things pass so quickly. The book of Ecclesiastes puts it like this: 'I hated all the things I had toiled for under the sun, because I must leave them to the one who comes after me. And who knows whether he will be a wise man or a fool?'[53] Numbering our days does not mean we don't work hard, or try to achieve great things. It means we put those things in the context of the whole of life – friends, family, God.

All of this was impressed strongly on Dr James Dobson some years ago. He recounts an incident that occurred whilst he was at Los Angeles Children's Hospital.

One of my colleagues died during my last year

at Children's Hospital, having served on our university medical faculty for more than 25 years. During his tenure as a professor, he had earned the respect and admiration of both professionals and patients, especially for his research findings and contributions to medical knowledge. This doctor had reached the pinnacle of success in his chosen field, and enjoyed the status and financial rewards that accompany such accomplishment. He had tasted every good thing, by the standards of the world.

At the next staff meeting following his death, a five-minute eulogy was read by a member of his department. Then the chairman invited the entire staff to stand, as is our custom in situations of this nature, for one minute of silence in memory of the fallen colleague. I have no idea what the other members of the staff contemplated during that 60-second pause, but I can tell you what was going through my mind.

I was thinking, 'Lord, is this what it all comes down to? We sweat and worry and labour to achieve a place in life, to impress our fellow men with our competence. We take ourselves so seriously, overreacting to the insignificant events of each passing day. Then finally, even for the brightest among us, all these experiences fade into history, and our lives are summarized with a five-minute eulogy and sixty seconds of silence. It hardly seems worth the effort, Lord.'[54]

So long as we only think of this life, we will spend it stamping and kicking to preserve our hold on it – our possessions, our opinions, our ambitions. But at the very best we only get seventy years or so.

> Death lays its icy hand on Kings;
> Sceptre and crown
> Must tumble down
> And in the dust be equal made
> With the poor crooked scythe and spade.[55]

An eastern monarch sent his wise men away to find a phrase that would fit every circumstance of life. They were gone for seven years but finally came back with it. You can write this phrase over buildings, circumstances, and our very lives – 'This, too, shall pass away.'

I have numbered my days. If God spares me to live to seventy I have seven thousand six hundred and sixty-five left. I cannot live every one of them as though it is my last – that would drive me and my friends crazy – but I can remember how short they are. And I can occasionally ask myself whether the things I am spending these days on are truly valuable, so that when I am old I will look back on them with satisfaction.

In my office I have a day-planner. It is made up of small boxes, each has a date in it, and every day I am pulled from one box into another; today is 16 March and it dragged me from yesterday and into its territory. There is however a box for me that has no doors. I will not go from there to the next date. It is the day I will die. Now here is the big question of the universe: Does that box have no doors because it is a coffin and death is the end? Or does it have no doors because it has no walls and death is a beginning?

Bertrand Russell, the atheistic philosopher, said, 'When I die I rot. There is darkness without and when I die there will be darkness within. Triviality for a moment, then nothing.' But from earliest times men and women have not believed that. When archaeologists discovered some of the oldest tombs on our planet they found the skeletons curled in a foetal position and encased in earthenware eggs; whoever had buried them was saying, 'One day you will live again.'

The story of Jesus is of somebody who had no fear of the final enemy. In fact he ruined every funeral he went to. He ruined Jairus' daughter's funeral, and the funeral of the young man who was restored to his widowed mother. He even ruined his own. Somebody had come into our world who had power over the last enemy. He could tell it when to go – he cried out towards a tomb in the hillside, 'Lazarus, come out!'[56] And he could tell it when to come – and so in his own death he 'gave up his spirit'.[57] He put it like this, '. . . I lay down my life – only to take it up again. No one takes it from me, but I lay it down of my own accord. I have authority to lay it down and authority to take it up again.'[58] The book of Hebrews says a fascinating thing of him: 'By embracing death, taking it into himself, he destroyed the Devil's hold on death and freed all who cower through life, *scared to death of death*.'[59]

As I read the New Testament I sometimes get the feeling that Paul, who had met the risen Christ, is actually taunting the grim reaper:

> Death swallowed by triumphant Life!
> Who got the last word, oh, Death?
> oh, Death, who's afraid of you now?[60]

Of course I'm apprehensive but I'm less afraid of death than I used to be. That is strange, for my grown children, aching limbs and greying hair, all whisper to me that the final enemy is getting nearer. But Christ is risen, the sting is drawn and death stands head down, robbed of victory. That knowledge has not stopped my grieving when I have lost somebody I love dearly; I miss them; sometimes I ache for them. But I do believe that death's victory is not final, and that the words John Donne wrote hundreds of years ago are prophetic indeed . . . *Death thou shalt die.*

For them it was only the beginning of the real story. All their life in this world . . . had only been the cover and title page: now at last they were beginning Chapter One of the Great Story which no one on earth has read: which goes on for ever: in which every chapter is better than the one before.[61]

C. S. Lewis, *The Last Battle*

10

You're not home yet

It was late on a Sunday evening that it happened. I had taken a group of teenagers on a beach barbeque but as they leapt from the cars to run to the sand one child lingered in the car. If only we had some warning of life-changing events perhaps we could get ready in some way for them, but that is not in their nature; such moments surprise us, sneak up on us, ambush us. It was so on this occasion.

Alicia, the girl who stayed, was fifteen and within six months would be dead. When she was fourteen she had contracted cancer. The chemotherapy had caused her hair to fall out, and when I sat with her that night it was just beginning to grow back; she looked stunning even with closely cropped hair. We could hear the sounds of shouts and screams in the distance as a typical youth group argued over who had found the largest piece of driftwood, but at that moment it was quiet in my car. I fumbled for something to say – 'Alicia, how are you coping with all this?'

And it was then that she said it. She had no idea what she was about to do; it did not enter her head that her words would be broadcast across the world, that radio and television would beam them to places she had never heard of. She did not know that men and women would catch their breath when they heard them, that people who had lost hope would be lifted.

I last spoke them recently in the trouble-torn city of Belfast in Northern Ireland. I stood on the stage of the brand-new Waterfront Centre, one of the finest concert halls in the world, in front of a packed audience. The spotlights were in my eyes and I couldn't make out the faces in the front row, let alone the thousands of others reaching right up into the gods. But I felt the faces, imagined the looks, sensed the emotion, caught a little of the hope as I shouted into the darkness beyond the lights the sentence that Alicia said to me that evening.

Alicia Owens said: '*I know where I'm going.*'

She was just fifteen and you may think her naive – but I don't. You may say, 'She had no idea of the pain ahead.' But she had already suffered much; she knew what lay ahead of her. No, the words of that child that night were not born out of shallowness, or immaturity. Alicia was looking the greatest enemy in the face and saying in her heart, 'You are not as fearsome as I first thought. You cannot hold me.'

As I drove home that night her words did not leave me. In fact, I think I knew even then that they never would. Alicia knew what kings and presidents do not know. She knew where she was going.

Was she deluded? I don't think so. She had decided that in this matter she was going to trust Christ. By any standards Jesus Christ is the most significant figure in the history of mankind. Einstein said of him, 'Here everything is extraordinary.' And what made him so extraordinary was that he had such a clear understanding of that other world. Philosophers have grasped for it; theologians have prayed to understand it; *he knew it.*

On the evening before he died he ate a meal with his disciples.[62] And it was at that meal he told them three things that brought their world crashing down around them. He said, 'One of you will betray me and one of you will deny me.' Imagine what it must have been like for them; just twelve and already there was a betrayer and a coward amongst them; but there was worse to come. He said, 'I am going to leave you, and where I am going you cannot come.' They had given up everything to follow him. They had left family and businesses, they had been ridiculed and honoured. They had seen him heal the blind and raise the dead. He had sent them out to do his work but when they came back he was always there for them. And now he was going.

When my son was small and I was about to leave the house he would always shout, 'Can I come with you?' Peter, the disciple, does the same. He says to Jesus, 'Where are you going that I can't come?' And it was then, when they were at one of the lowest points of their lives, that he began to talk to them about another world. It was a world he understood; he knew where he was going. And he talked of it in terms of home. 'In my father's house are many rooms, if it were not so I would have told you. I am going to get it ready for you. I want you to be with me.'

It was as if he was saying, 'You must grasp that other world. You will not make sense of this one unless you do. This is not all there is.' You and I were meant to live with one eye on heaven.

Some months after our conversation in the car and as Alicia lay very near to death, I held her hand and told her I was going to dedicate to her a book that I had just written, called *The Sixty Minute Father*. I said, 'It will be to Alicia Owens – who knew where she was going.' She was pleased and smiled and I was honoured to do it, but neither of us had any idea that all over the world people would ask me to tell the story of that teenager's faith and her certainty in a world more real than this.

Shortly after her death I was asked to speak on the BBC and told listeners about Alicia and read what seemed to capture the heart of her belief. It talks of death as our just passing over a horizon.

I am standing upon the seashore. A ship at my side spreads her white sails to the morning breeze and starts for the blue ocean. She is an object of beauty and strength, and I stand and watch her until at length she hangs like a speck of white cloud just where the sea and sky come down to mingle with each other. Then someone at my side says: 'There! She's gone.'

Gone where? Gone from my sight – that is all.

She is just as large in mast and hull and spar as she was when she left my side, and just as able to bear her load of living freight to the place of destination. Her diminished size is in me, not in her; and just at the moment when someone at my side says, 'There! She's gone,' there are other eyes watching her coming, and other voices ready to take up the glad shout, 'Look! She comes!'[63]

Some years ago a missionary was returning to America after working in Africa for forty years. He had never had a furlough and as the boat pulled into New York harbour he wondered if there would be anybody to meet him. And then he heard some music. He thought, 'How lovely, they've got together a little band for me.' But then he realised that President Roosevelt was on the boat returning from a four-week safari in Africa, and it wasn't a little band, it was a big band.

Because of the President he was delayed and when he eventually stepped on to the dockside it was empty – there was nobody there to meet him. He went to a little hotel and fell by his bed weeping. He cried out, 'God, this President has been four weeks on holiday in Africa and he gets such a welcome back; I have served you forty years and for me there is no welcome home.'

And then he felt a voice whisper in his heart: 'You're not home yet.'

It is no surprise that the life of faith is, at times, a battle. But in war we are sometimes wounded. At such times everything may scream out at us, 'Give up – you've done enough – nobody could blame you.' These feelings are neither unusual nor modern. The account of the life of Elijah tells the story of a man of faith, wisdom and incredible courage. It is the record of somebody unafraid of opposition, be that spiritual or physical. This man was not one to walk easily away from a challenge. And yet the time came for this great warrior of faith when he sat under a tree and said, 'You can take my life now – I've had enough.' I have sometimes sat under that tree and I think that occasionally you may have been there too.

I often thank God that the Bible is so honest about its heroes, and it is that very fact that encourages me to share a lesson with you that was carved out of some of the darkest times of my life.

11

Just occasionally – I can hide

I have often wondered what the psalmist was going through when he cried out, 'Why are you downcast, O my soul?'[64] Could it be that he was echoing an experience that others have attested to all through church history? Some have called it 'the dark night of the soul'. This is a time in our life when it seems that God, if he is there at all, is far away. We may be plagued by doubts about our faith, we find it hard to pray except to call out to God for help, but so often it seems that heaven is preoccupied.

One of the most difficult things about such a time is that while we are going through it, the world goes on. If we are church leaders, there are sermons to preach (and – even harder – to prepare), there are people to counsel and, irony of ironies, doubters to encourage. If we are involved in youth work, the fact that we are in a spiritual desert doesn't stop the kids turning up on a Monday night. If we are parents, our five-year-old still expects mum or dad to say prayers before bed. Life is going on; but we are dying inside.

In some ways we are glad life hasn't stopped and are grateful for the activity, for when we have gone through such times before, we have found that the sheer act of getting on with life has helped us get through it. But now it doesn't seem to be working; we feel we are losing our grip on our faith. The incredible thing is that so often at the moment of greatest doubt and deepest spiritual depression, our faith is more important to us than anything else. We *want* to feel close to God. We *want* to believe.

Some years ago a book was published with an inspired title: it was called *Honourably Wounded*.[65] The words referred to that category of soldiers in the last war who were discharged with full honour having suffered some injury in the service of their country. The author took up that theme and spoke of those who had suffered some hurt (often emotional breakdown) in Christian service. These faithful people had often served long and hard in trying to follow Christ but finally it seemed that their bodies had had enough, they could go on no longer; they were 'honourably wounded'.

Many Christians come into that category. I think of a young vicar and his wife. They had joined their new church with such enthusiasm and hope, firmly believing it was God's call on their lives. When I met with them they were broken, hurting and confused. It wasn't the battle against the forces of darkness that surprised them, rather the battleground which turned out to be *inside* the church they had come to lead. They were emotionally drained.

We are complicated beings and because of the very nature of the problem there are usually no easy answers. Such experiences are painful and at times excruciating in their intensity, but I doubt whether we can escape them completely. If we face them we can often find they produce a humility, and therefore a strength, that we might have lacked if the sun had never stopped shining. But it is not always necessary that they take us by surprise. When I have gone through those times I have often observed, looking back, that they did not come quite out of the blue, but that in fact there were circumstances that, had I been a little more perceptive, might have given a hint as to what might be around the corner. Let me mention two.

Criticism

Oscar Wilde was once sent a letter by a theatre critic after the opening night of one of his plays. It read: 'You did not send me a ticket for your opening night. Perhaps you will be good enough to send one for your second night – if you have one.'

Wilde sent a note back: 'Please find enclosed two tickets for my new play. One is for you and the other for a friend – if you have one.'

But it's not just playwrights that have to face the critics. Each of us must live our lives in front of those who are waiting to give their verdict on our performance. Our critics can be our greatest blessing and occasionally the opposite. The apostle Paul talks about this in his letter to the Christians who lived in Corinth.

I care very little if I am judged by you or by any human court; indeed, I do not even judge myself. My conscience is clear, but that does not make me innocent. It is the Lord who judges me. Therefore judge nothing before the appointed time; wait till the Lord comes. He will bring to light what is hidden in darkness and will expose the motives of men's hearts. At that time each will receive his praise from God.[66]

Paul is talking about the three critics that every one of us will have to face. Firstly there are other people. They will tell you that you are too rich or too poor, too sombre or too jolly. They will tender their evaluation of your parenting, your prayer-life and your waistline. Professor Lewis Smedes paraphrased Paul's attitude to his critics like this:

You will evaluate my conduct and you will make an assessment of me, I know, and when you do I will listen to you. I know that you will size up my work; when you do, I will consider what you say. What you say and what you think about me matters to me. But I want you to know that after I have wrestled with my own conscience, after I have consulted my own convictions, and after I

130

> have made my decisions, your judgement will not
> matter much. It matters some, but not much. I will
> not rest my case with you.[67]

That is a vital principle. We would be wise to listen to our critics, but you can't live life looking over your shoulder wondering what they are making of your efforts – to live like that is to be imprisoned. One woman said, 'I have spent fifty years – half a century – imprisoned by other people's opinions of my life.'

Some years ago a woman said to me, 'Wouldn't it be ironic, with you and Dianne involved in a family ministry, if your own children went off the rails?' I may have imagined it but I thought I detected in her voice a slight hope that they would. The truth is, it wouldn't be ironic at all. Dianne and I have made many mistakes, but we have given the task of parenting our best shot and I won't live my life tormented by the opinions of others. Many church leaders face this. Their children are not allowed to be like other people's children. Because they are the leader's children the congregation demand they behave five levels above normal – and it's wrong.

I have generally found that one's critics fall into two categories. Firstly there are those who criticise in the hope of building you up. They may be misguided but at heart they want your good. Listen to them, weigh what they say, and try their advice. These people will save you from tragedy, from making a fool of yourself, and enable you to become even more effective. Even if it hurts, *it's worth it*: 'Wounds from a friend can be trusted.'[68]

The second category criticise to bring you down. They do not have your long-term good at heart and they *enjoy* the criticism far too much. They will often preface biting remarks with lines like, 'I've got something I want to say to you in love,' or, 'You know how much I appreciate you, but lots of us are worried about . . .' They will rarely name the 'lots of us' and normally these are mythical characters that exist in the mind of the critic. You will find you can never please them, so don't try; they will wear you out. The last thing they want is for you to answer their difficulty because that would rob them of their ammunition. They are like the religious leaders of whom Jesus said, 'You are like children in the street playing games. You don't want to play weddings and you don't want to play funerals.'[69]

But according to Paul's list that leaves critic number two to deal with: ourselves. And it's here that Paul says a fascinating thing: 'I do not even judge myself. My conscience is clear, but that does not make me innocent.' Of course the Bible tells us that it's good to examine our hearts, but not too much, and sometimes not too seriously, because we can fool ourselves.

In our home we have some bathroom scales. You can put weight on or take it off depending on how you stand on them. If you want to lose weight you lean to the left and push hard on the back of your foot. This simple action does away with the need to jog or eat salads. If you need to put on a few pounds you lean forward and press down. We will never get rid of them; all you need for the perfect figure is a little balance and the innate ability we all have to fool ourselves.

Somebody reading this book will wake up tomorrow morning, take a look in the mirror and exclaim, 'What a great face! What a privilege for the world to see that face today.' Almost everything they do during the day will be successful and when they fall into bed at the end of yet another triumphant twenty-four hours they will smile and say to themselves, 'You were awesome today.' Somebody else, also at present reading this book, will wake up tomorrow morning and they too will look in the mirror. They will sigh softly, look to heaven and say, 'Lord, you must have had so many noses to choose from, did I have to end up with this one? And were you so very short on eyebrows?' They will feel that they fail at everything they touch that day, and finally they will slump into bed feeling that somehow real life has passed them by.

The fascinating thing is, in terms of what actually occurred, both those days may have been exactly the same, but the individuals involved see them from the perspective of quite different personalities. We view our lives through certain coloured spectacles. Some of us are too hard on ourselves and some could do with a little more self-criticism. Try to understand the kind of person you are and try to make your evaluations more objective. Some of us are plagued by negative thoughts. Some typical ones are:

I must not show any weakness in this situation.
I must always act so that others will like me.
Most people are out to get me.
If I am really me, people won't like me.
I do not deserve to relax.

This is so often a battle of the mind. The Bible says, 'We take captive every thought to make it obedient to Christ.'[70] That is, at the very least, a call to clear thinking which acknowledges a critic far higher than ourselves. And it is that third critic who is now waiting in the wings.

Paul says, 'It is the Lord who judges me.' One day the motives of every person's heart will be revealed and we will know for sure how we did. It is both sobering to realise that day will miss nothing, but it is also liberating to live in the knowledge of being judged by somebody who loves us completely.

The second issue that is so often at the heart of times of spiritual dryness is not very dramatic but that robs it of none of its potency to crush joy and peace from our lives.

Sheer tiredness

Many people today are exhausted. Often it is the accumulation of years in which we have tried to keep a myriad of activities going at once. We have been putting out chairs for the morning service, cutting sandwiches for the youth group and writing out new songs for the overhead projector at midnight on Saturday – and doing all of this whilst running a home, keeping down a job or perhaps dealing with the trauma of unemployment, and at the same time trying to tame a teenager. And we have just got tired.

Sometimes it's not until we try to relax that we realise how tired we are. I say 'try' because it's not that easy. Our body has got used to the thrill of adrenaline, and so we find it hard to sit still. We need to be active and, who would have believed it – we get ill on holiday. We wait all year for a summer break and for the first three days we are holed up in a bedroom on the Costa del Sol or, even more typically, we find that we *always* get 'flu at Christmas.

Most of us identify with this but there is another kind of tiredness, perhaps even a weariness, that can settle on us and make it hard to press on. Let me take you back for a moment to the psalmist and to something else he wrote at a time of incredible pressure. Before we read it let me remind you about this man. It was he who had taken on Goliath and won. Since that day he had fought battles for God that made the tussle against the giant seem trivial. He had battled against overwhelming odds both inside and outside the kingdom that had won his allegiance. He had faced treachery, betrayal and disappointment, but he was a man of courage and he had battled hard. David was a fighter.

But one day he wrote this: 'I will take refuge in

the shadow of your wings until the disaster has passed.'[71] The image is the one Jesus used when he wept over Jerusalem: it is of a mother hen who suddenly senses danger. She spreads her wings wide and calls her little ones to run to her for safety. David says, 'God, do that for me. I have fought hard and long but I can't go on like this. Hide me in the shadow of your wings.' This is not a fighting image – you cannot win battles from this position – but it is a place of restoration, of peace, of safety; and it is for a season.

I have discovered in my life that there have been times when I could not go on as I had been. There have been occasions when I have heard Jesus say to me, 'Come apart and rest awhile.' My protests have sometimes been strong, 'But the crowds are still wanting us, and the Gospel is still to be preached, and there are so many needs.' At such times I have sometimes felt his smile, not of reproof but rather of amusement, that I should have believed the responsibility for the whole kingdom sat squarely on my shoulders and that the God of whom it is written, 'And God said, "Let there be light," *and there was light*,'[72] would find it hard to manage without me for a while.

At such times I have sat down with a cup of coffee and considered whether there are demands from which I could be released for a time. Sometimes this has involved going to colleagues and telling them openly how I am feeling and asking for their help. To do so I have had to battle with inner voices that whispered to me 'But they're under pressure too,' and, most of all, with my pride.

Such times have meant that I have said 'No' to things in which I would loved to have been involved. I have sometimes cancelled things to create some space where I can breathe a little. On one occasion I was able to take a short break from the church leadership team that I was part of.

It was at such a time that a friend, observing a life of frenzied activity, said to me, 'You seem to have lost the ability to spend time with yourself.' He suggested that once a week I go for a walk to a nearby park and just 'kick the leaves'. He counselled me not to take a pen with which to jot down seminar ideas that might come to me, or even to feel the pressure to pray, but just to practise spending time with . . . me.

It seemed at first indulgent, and I would sometimes look around furtively to check whether the approaching jogger was somebody from our church who might be surprised that I had so much time on my hands. (It didn't occur to me that I might ask how come he had so much time on *his* hands!) But it wasn't just the guilt but rather that at first I found *I just couldn't do it.*

I had spent so much of my life 'doing' that just 'being' was proving harder than I thought. But we can learn, and 'kicking the leaves' became, for me, a phrase that summed up the art of creating space for ourselves – not just for our sakes, but so that we may be effective in the task to which God has called us. I believe the reason so many of us find it hard to spend time with God in silence or in prayer is that we have lost the ability to spend time with *ourselves*. We are busy people, we love activity, we cannot be still.

But a lifestyle of furious activity means the experience of what some call 'burn-out' may be not far from us. It is a picture of a match burned to the end of the wood, of a candle struggling bravely to keep a light alive but the wick is almost gone, or, in more modern terms, of a rocket engine that went off the launching pad with such force but fell away quickly, its energy expended. Somebody once said, 'Give me a busy life any day! I would rather burn out than rust out!' The truth is, you and I were meant to do neither. We were meant to 'last out' – to finish the course – not drop out exhausted after two laps. We were meant to complete the journey, be it long or short.

'I will take refuge in the shadow of your wings until the disaster has passed.'

Enjoy it. You may be there shorter than you think.

The world is filled with people who have lost heart. You can sometimes see it in the eyes of old people who sit next to a pile of rubble after the devastation of an earthquake; they have no more tears. Occasionally you see that look of resignation in the eyes of a child who has never known the most simple encouragement.

To lose heart is often a precursor to losing life itself, for we lose the very will to live. And I have often seen those eyes of despair in the faces of the followers of Jesus. Somebody, some circumstance, or just the sheer accumulation of years of hardship has caused them to lose heart.

If this is how you feel then I want to help you to find heart again. If you were in my home I would sit you in my favourite chair, the one next to the fire, and I would try with all my heart to encourage you to keep pressing on. I wouldn't for a moment try to explain away, or dismiss, all you have been through that may have robbed you of joy but I would want to lift your head and most of all I would want to tell you how precious you are to God.

I pray with all my heart that for somebody, today, this last lesson will be rain in the desert.

12

Don't lose heart

I once lost heart in dramatic fashion. I noticed that our local leisure club was to hold a Tuesday 'keep fit' evening. I should have deduced from the title that it was designed for those who wanted to retain what they had already achieved, rather than for those for whom the concept was only a dream. That detail was lost on me and I went.

My son lent me a pair of trainers and I found a pair of tracksuit bottoms that I last used in form five at school. They seemed to have shrunk a little but nevertheless I donned the kit and set off.

The room was full. I have never seen such tiny waists and so much Lycra concentrated into such a small floor area. These creatures were rippling fitness. The instructor introduced herself and I stood listening whilst vainly trying to hold my stomach in and, at the same time, attempting to retrieve the cord of my joggers which had disappeared into the waistband.

She distributed tasks around the room and left me until

last. It seemed she had decided I needed a little personal tuition. She told me she wanted to test my basic fitness before launching me on the terrors that most of the other Lycra wearers were now engaged in. She took my pulse and then asked me to leap up and down on what looked like a small orange box. I kept this up for all of a minute and then, seeing the colour in my face and fearing the worst, she asked me to stop. She waited a short while and then took my pulse again.

Apparently if one is reasonably fit one's pulse returns to normal within two to three minutes. Mine came back on the following Thursday afternoon.

I had literally lost heart. If you had asked me to perform the simplest of functions when I had got off the orange box I couldn't have. With all the good will in the world *there was nothing left to give.*

Over the years I have observed and, at times, experienced some of the things that cause us to lose heart; I want to mention two in particular.

The power of the past

The first is being dogged by the past. Dianne and I were engaged when I was twenty-one. I had just finished college and was penniless. And that wouldn't have been such a problem if I hadn't needed to buy an engagement ring. Now if I were counselling my own children in that situation I would advise that they get a job and save for the ring, and, in so doing, they will make the experience more precious and more meaningful. It's good advice but it discounts the irrationality of love. I went to my bank manager.

Since that fateful day I have often had to deal with bank managers, and I think I could easily write a book entitled, *Bank Managers – Lessons I Wish I'd Learnt Earlier*. But in those days I was a trifle naive in such matters. I'm not sure what I expected, but perhaps thought he might say, 'In love! How splendid! A penniless student – ideal! How much would you like?' Instead he smiled at me. It wasn't a warm, encouraging smile – rather the forced, wind-like smile of one who was about to say, 'If you don't get out of my bank fast, I'll call security.'

I borrowed the money elsewhere and we bought a second-hand ring. One year later we bought a wedding band in a discount jeweller's, and we were married. Shortly after I qualified as a lawyer I bought Dianne an eternity ring. Those rings held such memories for us.

Last year was our twenty-fifth wedding anniversary and we were on holiday with our children and some friends. The rest of us had been in the sea for some time when Dianne joined us. And it was then it happened. She threw a ball to me and suddenly something flashed in the sunlight. I watched as three rings, as if in slow motion, left Dianne's hand. They seemed to hover in the air for a moment and then disappeared into the sea. At the same time, she shouted, 'My rings!' and I saw a look of utter grief on her face. I know that in the great sweep of life there are things a lot bigger than losing a little jewellery, but it was more than that: it was the memories, the emotion that those things held – and they were gone.

Of course we searched, but the sea was rough and our efforts were futile. For days afterwards I walked along the edge of the water half expecting to see them lying there waiting to be reclaimed. We never did get those rings back. I often think of them lying somewhere, or perhaps by now on other hands, but still full of our memories. If they could talk they would tell how they have heard times of helpless laughter, and of crying that seemed to come from the very soul. In short, they hold the memories of two lives, each with successes and failures. If I am wise I will learn lessons from that past but in another sense I must let go of it and move on.

Our yesterdays have a strange power over us. One way they can cause us to lose heart is if we believe the future can never be as good as the past. As we look back it seems the summers were hotter, the trains more reliable, and life better in almost every way. In such a mood we can yearn for our church to be like it used to be, our teenagers to be toddlers again, and society to be as it was. Of course there may be sense in wanting those things, but the book of Ecclesiastes has in it a fascinating warning, 'Do not say, "Why were the old days better than these?" For it is not wise to ask such questions.'[73] The past can trap us because it seems so good – we are tied to it. We refuse to face tomorrow because the memories of yesterday are so sweet.

Many a church leader is weary of people telling him

or her how wonderful church used to be, many a child is tired of a parent reminding her how perfect her sister was when she was that age, and lots of people never move into new experiences because in their hearts they continually hanker after 'how it used to be'. The past may have been wonderful but usually it wasn't as great as our memory makes out, and in any event *it is still the past.* Mark Twain said, 'Plan for the future, it's where you're going to spend the rest of your life.'

But there is another problem of the past, and it is the opposite one. Some of us cannot face tomorrow because we are haunted by our yesterdays. With us it is not the problem of yearning for the years that have gone, but never being able to forget them. They remind us of sorrow and pain, perhaps failure and crushing disappointment. You may feel like that now. There is so much in life you would love to do but you crouch like a rabbit suddenly caught in the headlights of a car, unable to move forward or back. Because of the hurt or failure of the past you have lost the confidence to go on.

The story of the Bible is of God using ordinary men and women who achieved what they did in spite of, and not because of, what they were. Many of them had known pasts with shame and failure in them but they experienced the truth of a fascinating promise God gave Israel. That nation had known years of spiritual barrenness but he said to them, 'And I will restore to you the years that the locusts have eaten.'[74]

Imagine what it was like the day the locusts came. One moment the fields were full of wheat blowing in the wind and then you heard the sound. And after the sound came the darkness, as if the sun itself had given up in the face of the devastation that swept across the land. And when they were gone there was only ruin. The preparation, the sowing, the careful tending – all wasted. The hope of the harvest was dead.

Most of us go through a time in our lives when we identify with this. The years have taken their toll of us. We look back on disappointment, failure and heartache. We believe our life has been devastated. Such a situation may come about for many reasons. We may be victims of the wrongs of others, or our own wrongs may have caused us to pay a price we would never have imagined. It may be that illness or disappointments in our family have consumed our thoughts and drained us of effort. But God can change our lives; he can restore to us the years the locust has eaten.

This does not mean that suddenly life becomes easy, but it does mean that tomorrow does not have to be like yesterday. The times of darkness and nights of tears, the memories of past failure need not imprison us forever. This is true even if that devastation is because we have been foolish; even if the responsibility lies just with us. He is a God of new beginnings.

I was regretting the past
And fearing the future . . .
Suddenly my Lord was speaking:
'MY NAME IS I AM.' He paused.
I waited. He continued.

'WHEN YOU LIVE IN THE PAST
WITH ITS MISTAKES AND REGRETS
IT IS HARD. I AM NOT THERE.
MY NAME IS NOT *I WAS*.

WHEN YOU LIVE IN THE FUTURE
WITH ITS PROBLEMS AND FEARS
IT IS HARD. I AM NOT THERE.
MY NAME IS NOT *I WILL BE*.

WHEN YOU LIVE IN THIS MOMENT
IT IS NOT HARD
I AM HERE.
MY NAME IS *I AM*.'[75]

When nothing makes sense

But even if we deal with our past there is another issue
that time and time again forces us to lose heart. The clue
to it is in something Paul wrote to the Christians who
lived at Corinth:

> We are hard pressed on every side, but not
> crushed; perplexed, but not in despair; perse-
> cuted, but not abandoned; struck down, but not
> destroyed.[76]

That's quite a list, but I think, of all those difficulties, the
hardest to bear may have been '*perplexed*'. The literal

meaning is 'at a loss as to know how to go on'. When you are hard pressed you know you are in a battle, when you are persecuted you can see the enemy, being struck down is a terrible thing, but at least you know where the blow came from. But 'perplexed'?

This is a time when we don't understand what is going on. It may even be a time when it appears God has left us, let us down, or in our lowest moments seems even to have betrayed us. It could be in the area of our prayer life. We had honestly believed God was going to answer our prayers with a resounding 'Yes!' The person we prayed for was so precious and we desperately wanted him to be well. And there were so many encouraging signs. We prayed the operation would be successful and it seemed to be; we prayed through every day of the treatment, and, as time went by, we had a growing sense that all would be well. But our friend died. We accepted it, we even explained it to others, but in our own heart was a deep sense of perplexity and, if we were honest, a little anger.

Another root of perplexity may lie in disappointment as to what we have achieved in our ministry – in our work for God. It may be that as well as our job in the factory we have given time to teenagers. But the youth group that we used to lead is now scattered, and whereas at one time we believed these young men and women were going to grow into strong faith in Christ, it now appears they are not interested. When we meet them in the street they seem embarrassed and mumble their reasons why they don't come to church any more. We look at a younger set of teens waiting to join our group and we wonder if we've got the stamina to do it all again when there seems so little fruit for our labours.

It may be you are a church leader. When you accepted the invitation to join your church you were sure that it was of God. The people were welcoming, they promised to help with housing and babysitting, and constantly told you that God had answered their prayers in sending you. The honeymoon lasted six months: they never did get you the house they promised, they didn't manage babysitting beyond the first week, and it seems the only way God will answer their current prayers is for you to be called to another church. It has all gone so very wrong.

You honestly believed the change of job was God's will for your life. It was abroad, in fact in Africa, and you went willingly, but after six months you became ill and had to return. You are devastated, embarrassed and perplexed.

You prayed so hard for your husband to find the faith that has so changed your life. Finally he agreed to come to church with you. To say it was an off-day would be an understatement. The preacher, who is normally compelling, seemed half-asleep, the drama was embarrassing and the welcome committee looked like piranhas in suits. When you got home he swore never to bother again.

There are no easy answers to such situations but part of the answer may lie in a sermon I heard when I was a teenager: the heart of it remains with me thirty years later. The preacher talked about 'the non-fairy tale ending of the will of God'. He said that in life today happy endings are mandatory, but God sometimes looks at things from a different perspective. He takes a longer view; he is not in so much of a hurry as we are and, furthermore, he has a way of achieving things through brokenness that are harder to craft when we feel all is well. For that very reason we cannot say to the person who had to return from Africa after just one month, 'Ah, it obviously wasn't God's will for you to go there.' It may just have been God's perfect will.

Even more sobering is the fact that we cannot look at times of our life when things seems to be going well and presume we are therefore in the centre of God's will. If you are a business person be careful of saying, 'I must be doing what I should, look how my business is prospering.' His ways are higher than ours and his thoughts higher than our thoughts.

And we may be perplexed because of personal circumstances. Our family life may be very difficult, our children are a disappointment to us or we are in financial difficulty. It may be that we are a single person and our career is not going well – in fact we have been demoted, our friendships seem awkward and unfulfilling. Life is not good. It is easy at such times to lose heart and in so doing to lose our faith in God.

Those of us brought up in the Western world have been infected with a belief that makes all of this especially difficult. This belief is quite different to that taught to the majority of Christians through church history, and yet in our culture it seems so fitting. It is simply that God exists to make us happy. When life goes well we feel close to him, when it goes badly we feel distant. And it is right here that one of the most fascinating of Jesus' parables may have something to say to us. 'Some [seed] fell on rocky places, where it did not have much soil. It sprang up quickly, because the soil was shallow. But when the sun came up, the plants were scorched, and they withered because they had no root.'[77] The sun speaks of persecution, of hard times, and the fascinating thing is that the same sun that caused the good seed to grow caused the seed in shallow ground to die. Somebody says, 'Since I became a Christian, life has got worse, my family is going through a difficult time, my business is suffering, I can't go on in this faith.' And somebody else in even worse circumstances says, 'Thank God that I know him; if I didn't I could never get through it all.'

Not all our prayers will be answered with 'Yes'. Not all our children will turn out as we want, not all our churches will grow as we had hoped, and most of us will know times of crushing doubt. If you and I are to finish the course we are somehow going to have to learn how to hold on to God when our circumstances scream at us that there is no good reason to do so. This is not a new experience. Habakkuk wrote over three thousand years ago of this very period in our lives. This was his response:

> Though the fig-tree does not bud
>   and there are no grapes on the vines,
> though the olive crop fails
>   and the fields produce no food,
> though there are no sheep in the pen
>   and no cattle in the stalls,
> yet I will rejoice in the LORD.[78]

This is not an easy-believism joy. This is not frivolous. This is not easy. This is faith that is tried whilst standing by a grave, or in unemployment, or when our children are breaking our hearts; it is faith that rises out of the ashes of our deepest disappointments. Sometimes at our lowest moments this faith sneaks up on us because we have nowhere else to go, and as surely as night follows day every one of us will come to a place at some time in our lives where we go on believing, not just because God seems good to us, but in spite of the most crushing perplexity. At that moment alongside the giant of doubt comes the child of faith that ultimately looks up and cries, 'I don't understand but I still trust you.' At our lowest moments it may even allow us to cry out with Job, 'Though he slay me, yet will I hope in him.'[79]

At the moment we 'see but a poor reflection as in a mirror'[80] but one day we will have perfect vision and understanding. And remember, when we stand before him there will be some surprises. The work we did that seemed so fruitless may look a little different from that perspective; the disappointments of today may take on a different colour in five years' time, but perhaps even more so from the view of another world. And who knows what changes may be in store for the child who today breaks our heart; perhaps in parenting, as in life, we shouldn't read the score at half-time.

Well, the lessons I wished I'd learnt earlier are declared. They are lessons of life and death and of that other world. They are experiences that have convinced me that in spite of who I am inside, God is not finished with me yet.

One woman put it like this:

'I know it all and I still love you.' That is the convincing, convicting, liberating truth that comes from an encounter with Christ. 'All is known. There is no need to pretend any more.' I wrestled with that truth, but it is hard to lay aside a mask when it looks so like you and you have worn it so long that you can't remember what you looked like without it.[81]

Oh those masks, that hide the real us from others, and even from ourselves. Like the circus clown we smile whilst our hearts are breaking:

I have played the part so long,
Worn the make-up and the smile.
Took the bow and the applause,
Said, 'Oh fine, oh, yes, of course . . . I'm fine.'

> Donned the costume, trod the boards,
> Learnt the lines and sung the song,
> Made you laugh and made you cry.
> I have done it all so long . . .
>
> I have done it all so long
> That I don't expect you see
> That to get this leading role,
> The real cost was . . . me.[82]

You can take the mask off. God loves you. That is the simple, irrational truth. It is true if you feel him so close you could reach out and touch him. It is true if, at this moment, you are in deep despair and he seems so very distant. It is true if you have no love for him, or if you have lost the love that was once so dear to you. God loves you.

Our time together is almost over, but let me ask you to do something that I believe could be very significant. Following this chapter is an excerpt from Paul's letter to the church at Rome. Can I encourage you not to skip it, but to make yourself a cup of coffee, sit in your favourite armchair and, as you meditate on it, let its wisdom and challenge seep into your spirit? It seems to me so clearly to sum up the heart of the Christian faith. If this passage becomes our life goal we may not attain it all, but we will look back when we are old and be satisfied; and whatever our past, we can, by God's grace, begin to live these principles *today*.

There are many writings which have inspired me but the following two pieces are amongst my favourite prose in the whole world. The first comes from John White and is from the introduction to his book, *The Fight*. It sums up so much of what we have considered together:

> As you live the Christian life, you may have periods of darkness or of doubt. You may encounter painful struggle and discouragement. But there will also be moments of exultation and glory. And most important of all, you will become free.[83]

And the second is from the words of Paul, the man who had such a keen sense of his own frailty, but who eventually fought a good fight, and who by God's grace finished the course.

> Therefore we do not lose heart. Though outwardly we are wasting away, yet inwardly we are being renewed day by day. For our light and momentary troubles are achieving for us an eternal glory that far outweighs them all. So we fix our eyes not on what is seen, but on what is unseen. For what is seen is temporary, but what is unseen is eternal.[84]

Don't ever give up.

Lessons of life from the letter to the Romans

So here's what I want you to do, God helping you:
Take your everyday, ordinary life – your sleeping,
eating, going-to-work, and walking-around life –
and place it before God as an offering. Embracing
what God does for you is the best thing you
can do for him. Don't become so well adjusted
to your culture that you fit into it without even
thinking. Instead, fix your attention on God. You'll
be changed from the inside out.

Readily recognize what he wants from you, and
quickly respond to it. Unlike the culture around you,
always dragging you down to its level of immaturity, God brings the best out of you, develops
well-formed maturity in you.

I'm speaking to you out of deep gratitude for all
that God has given me, and especially as I have
responsibilities in relation to you. Living then, as
every one of you does, in pure grace, it's important
that you not misinterpret yourselves as people who
are bringing this goodness to God. No, God brings
it all to you. The only accurate way to understand
ourselves is by what God is and by what he does for
us, not by what we are and what we do for him.

In this way we are like the various parts of a
human body. Each part gets its meaning from the
body as a whole, not the other way round. The
body we're talking about is Christ's body of chosen
people. Each of us finds our meaning and function

as a part of his body. But as a chopped-off finger or cut-off toe we wouldn't amount to much, would we? So since we find ourselves fashioned into all these excellently formed and marvellously functioning parts in Christ's body, let's just go ahead and be what we were made to be, without enviously or proudly comparing ourselves with each other, or trying to be something we aren't.

If you preach, just preach God's Message, nothing else; if you help, just help, don't take over; if you teach, stick to your teaching; if you give encouraging guidance, be careful that you don't get bossy; if you're put in charge, don't manipulate; if you are called to give aid to people in distress, keep your eyes open and be quick to respond; if you work with the disadvantaged, don't let yourself get irritated or depressed by them. Keep a smile on your face.

Love from the centre of who you are; don't fake it. Run for dear life from evil; hold on for dear life to good. Be good friends who love deeply; practise playing second fiddle.

Don't burn out; keep yourselves fuelled and aflame. Be alert servants of the Master, cheerfully expectant. Don't quit in hard times; pray all the harder. Help needy Christians; be inventive in hospitality.

Bless your enemies; no cursing under your breath. Laugh with your happy friends when they're happy; share tears when they're down. Get along with each other; don't be stuck up. Make friends with nobodies; don't be the great somebody. Don't hit back; discover beauty in everyone. If you've got it in you, get along with everybody. Don't insist on getting even; that's not for you to do. 'I'll do the judging,' says God. 'I'll take care of it.'

Our scriptures tell us that if we see our enemy hungry, we are to go and buy that person lunch, or if he's thirsty, get him a drink. Your generosity will surprise him with goodness. Don't let evil get the best of you; get the best of evil by doing good.[85]

Oh, the depth of the riches of the wisdom and
    knowledge of God!
How unsearchable his judgments,
    and his paths beyond tracing out!
'Who has known the mind of the Lord?
    Or who has been his counsellor?'
'Who has ever given to God,
    that God should repay him?'
For from him and through him and to him are
    all things.
    To him be the glory for ever! Amen.[86]

Acknowledgments

Every effort has been made to locate sources and to seek permission for the use of quotes. In cases where this has not been possible, we apologise and will do all we can to rectify the situation in subsequent editions.

Chapter 1: The greatest freedom is in having nothing to prove

1. Materials from *When I Relax I Feel Guilty* (Chariot Victor Publishing, 1979). Used by permission.
2. Personal correspondence.
3. From an article in *Leadership* journal.
4. Henri Nouwen, *The Genesee Diary* (Doubleday, 1989).

Chapter 2: I am known completely and loved unconditionally

5. Personal correspondence.
6. Allan Ahlberg, 'Picking Teams', *Please Mrs Butler – Verses by Allan Ahlberg* (Puffin, 1983). Reproduced by permission of Frederick Warne & Co.

7. Romans 8:38–9 (paraphrased).
8. Jeff Lucas, *Walking Backwards* (Scripture Union, 1997). Used by permission.

Chapter 3: Tomorrow belongs to the failures

9. Annie Johnson Flint, 'He Giveth More Grace'.
10. John 15:5 (New King James version).
11. Matthew 14:22–33.
12. Luke 22:60–2.
13. Luke 22:31–2.
14. Acts 4:20.
15. Psalms 50:10–12.
16. Luke 2:41–50.
17. Luke 2:44–5 (Authorised Version).

Chapter 4: When you play to your strengths the giants fall faster

18. 1 Samuel 17:26ff.
19. John 6:15 (paraphrased).
20. Luke 12:13–14 (paraphrased).
21. Mark 1:37–8 (paraphrased).
22. 1 Corinthians 12:17.
23. Donald Clifton and Paula Nelson, *Play to your Strengths: Focus on what you do best and success will follow* (Piatkus, 1994).

Chapter 5: My Father is the gardener

24. 1 Corinthians 1:27–9.
25. Based on John 6:1–13.
26. C. S. Lewis, *The Four Loves* (HarperCollins).

Chapter 6: I was meant to party with my enemies

27. John 13:1ff.
28. John 13:14.
29. John 13:34.
30. 1 Corinthians 1 from Eugene Peterson, *The Message* (Navpress, 1993).
31. John 17:11.
32. James 4:11 (Peterson).
33. With thanks to Dave Phillips, Focus on the Family, Canada. Author unknown.
34. By Milton Olsen, publication unknown.
35. John 17:1–21.

Chapter 7: The kiss of God

36. See Psalms 103:12.
37. Luke 7:36–50.
38. John Bunyan, *The Pilgrim's Progress*.
39. Luke 15:11–32.
40. Luke 11:4 (paraphrased).
41. Matthew 18:23–35.

42. Luke 23:34.
43. Luke 23:42.
44. Luke 23:43.
45. Gwilym Hiraethog (translated by Robert Lowry), 'Here is Love'.

Chapter 8: Sometimes answers aren't the last word

46. Matthew 27:30.
47. Matthew 27:46.
48. Job 38:1–40:5 (paraphrased).

Chapter 9: Death will die

49. Ecclesiastes 3:8.
50. Ecclesiastes 3:2.
51. Psalms 90:10.
52. Psalms 90:12.
53. Ecclesiastes 2:18–19.
54. James Dobson, News from Focus on the Family.
55. J. Shirley, 'Death the Leveller', *The Golden Treasury* (Oxford University Press, 1964).
56. John 11:43.
57. John 19:30.
58. John 10:17–18.
59. Hebrews 2:14–15 (Peterson).
60. 1 Corinthians 15:55 (Peterson).

61. C. S. Lewis, *The Last Battle* (HarperCollins).

Chapter 10: You're not home yet

62. John 13:8–14:4.
63. Author unknown.

Chapter 11: Just occasionally – I can hide

64. Psalms 42:5.
65. Marjory Foyle, *Honourably Wounded* (Monarch).
66. 1 Corinthians 4:3–5.
67. Lewis Smedes, *How Can It be All Right When Everything is Wrong?* (Lion, 1982).
68. Proverbs 27:6.
69. Luke 7:32 (paraphrased).
70. 2 Corinthians 10:5.
71. Psalms 57:1.
72. Genesis 1:3.

Chapter 12: Don't lose heart

73. Ecclesiastes 7:10 (Authorised Version).
74. Joel 2:25 (Authorised Version).
75. Helen Mallicoat, 'I Am', in Tim Hansel, *Holy Sweat* (Word, 1987), p. 136.
76. 2 Corinthians 4:8–9.
77. Matthew 13:5.
78. Habakkuk 3:17–18.

79. Job 13:15.
80. 1 Corinthians 13:12.
81. Sheila Walsh, *Honestly* (Hodder & Stoughton, 1996). Used by permission.
82. Poem by Rob Parsons.
83. John White, *The Fight* (Inter-Varsity Press, 1977).
84. 2 Corinthians 4:16–18.
85. Romans 12 (Peterson).
86. Romans 11:33–6.